Making Animals Public

Inside the ABC's natural history archive

Making Animals Public

Inside the ABC's natural history archive

Gay Hawkins and Ben Dibley

SYDNEY UNIVERSITY PRESS

First published by Sydney University Press
© Gay Hawkins and Ben Dibley 2024
© Sydney University Press 2024

Reproduction and communication for other purposes
Except as permitted under Australia's *Copyright Act 1968*, no part of this edition may be reproduced, stored in a retrieval system, or communicated in any form or by any means without prior written permission. All requests for reproduction or communication should be made to Sydney University Press at the address below:

Sydney University Press
Gadigal Country
Fisher Library F03
University of Sydney NSW 2006
Australia
sup.info@sydney.edu.au
sydneyuniversitypress.com.au

 A catalogue record for this book is available from the National Library of Australia.

ISBN 9781743329719 paperback
ISBN 9781743329696 epub
ISBN 9781743329702 pdf

Cover image: David Parer filming King Penguins at Lusitania Bay, Macquarie Island, 1975 © D. Parer & E. Parer-Cook.

Cover design: Nathan Grice.

We acknowledge the traditional owners of the lands on which Sydney University Press is located, the Gadigal people of the Eora Nation, and we pay our respects to the knowledge embedded forever within the Aboriginal Custodianship of Country.

Contents

Acknowledgements	vii
Introduction *Crafting televisual animals*	1
Part One: Capturing	25
1 Cages and cameras *Screen animals before television*	29
2 Captivating viewers *Early natural history television on the ABC*	45
Part Two: Provoking	67
3 Developing the natural history genre *How animals and the media apparatus interact*	71
4 Making-of documentaries *Turning working animals into natural history animals*	93
Part Three: Inhabiting	115
5 The *Nature of Australia* series *Nationing nature*	119
6 After nature, after animals *Inhabiting a damaged planet*	137
Conclusion *Political animals*	163
References	177
Index	187

Acknowledgements

The research for this book was funded by the Australian Research Council's Linkage Program, Project ID LP130100465. The project was undertaken in partnership with the ABC. We wish to thank Kim Dalton, Director of Television, and Michael Brealey, Head of Strategy and Governance, for their enthusiastic support in the design and development of the application. Their commitment to investigating the role and impacts of the ABC on building audience interest in natural history and Australian animals and environments was significant.

Dr Morgan Richards played a critical role in the design of the project and the preparation of the grant. Her work on David Attenborough and the BBC Natural History Unit was invaluable. Fergus Grealy offered essential administrative support during the establishment of the grant at the Centre for Critical and Cultural Studies, University of Queensland.

During archival research at the ABC, Mary Jane Stannus, Head of Content Services, provided exceptional access to the archives and ongoing support and advice. So too did Natasha Marfutenko and Guy Tranter. We thank them all for their assistance and the work they have done maintaining the incredible archival and content resources of the ABC. Staff at the ABC's Natural History Archive at Ripponlea in Melbourne were equally helpful and facilitated access to a huge range of documents from the Natural History Unit.

Kathleen Phillips played a critical role in the initial stages of the project, documenting animals represented on early ABC radio and television programs and doing essential visual research into the Natural History Unit's huge collection of programs.

At different stages of the project, colleagues read draft chapters and offered very useful feedback. Thanks to Felicity Collins, Mike Michael and our colleagues Tony Bennett and Katherine Gibson at the Institute for Culture and Society at Western Sydney University for their generous feedback and insights.

A brief summary of the book's historical argument appeared in *The Conversation* (20 November 2019) as "Natural history on TV: how the ABC took Australian animals to the people". An earlier version of Chapter 1 was published as "Capturing spectral beasts: marsupial performances of the cinematic undead" in *Australian Humanities Review* (2020) 67. Parts of Chapter 2 were published as "Making animals public: early wildlife television and the emergence of environmental nationalism on the ABC" in *Continuum* (2019) 33(6). Chapter 4 draws on "Provoking animal realities on TV: exploring the affinities between STS and screen studies" published in *Science, Technology, & Human Values* (2020) 46(4).

Introduction
Crafting televisual animals

Soon after the invention of "the box", a new species was observed roaming across the small screen: televisual animals. Their origins and behaviours were complex. Partly a product of exhibitionary practices that had emerged in zoos, museums and cinema, these televisual animals were primarily the result of the strange media ecology that was early television. This ecology supported animals that were extraordinarily dynamic and expressive, narrated and usually set to music. It also nurtured animals perfectly naturalised to fit the medium and happy to perform on cue for the pleasure and edification of their human observers. For if this new species hadn't been convincing and fun to watch, it certainly wouldn't have survived in the extreme conditions of television.

Today there are many different subspecies under the broad category of "televisual animals". Consider the long evolution of Disney animals and their imperative to be cute, animated and funny, or the grand tradition of wildlife TV and its showcasing of animals that are timeless and spectacular. Then there are the apex predators hunting and killing for ratings, or political animals posing questions about human exploitation and abuse. The list goes on. What it shows is that the only thing these subspecies really have in common is their shared habitat: television. After that, it's the differences that really matter: the myriad techniques and mediations used to turn the material reality of an animal into a televisual reality; the different interactions and contact zones televisual animals generate with audiences; and the multiplicity of concerns that make these animals public and also make publics interested in looking at them.

The particular subspecies under investigation here is the "natural history animal", a unique breed usually sighted in pristine natural settings with little evidence of human civilisation.[1] More specifically, we're interested in natural history animals that began inhabiting the Australian Broadcasting Corporation's (ABC) television service soon after it first went to air in 1956.[2] Other animals in related media environments will also be investigated, but our primary focus is the cultural and political evolution of the ABC natural history animal. Like the British Broadcasting Corporation (BBC), the ABC was the product of a governmental commitment to building a broadcasting institution in the interests of informing, educating and entertaining populations. These commitments were seen as essential to the effective operation of a democratic national culture. Animals were implicated in this governmental project from the very beginning. The ABC's inaugural moment began with an animal soundscape. The first national radio broadcast in July 1932 started with the song of a lyrebird that filled living rooms and drew people to their radio sets.[3] As ABC radio audiences grew, listeners encountered talk about animals in everything from news bulletins, to rural programs, to the children's hour. The type of talk was immensely varied: information about cattle prices, how to manage diseases in sheep, stories and songs with animal characters and sounds, a naturalist describing the insect life in his backyard. In these soundscapes, mediated animals became present and palpable on radio, inhabiting listeners' everyday lives and imaginations.

The introduction of television in 1956 was a major shift in the institutional ecology of the ABC. TV meant that animals could now

---

1   Bousé 2000, 14–15.
2   The ABC became a corporation on 1 July 1983. Prior to that it was the Australian Broadcasting Commission. Although funded by the government, it is an independent statutory authority operating under the provisions of the *Australian Broadcasting Corporation Act 1983*.
3   Australian Broadcasting Commission, *Annual Report*, 1933.

Introduction

be *seen* and heard; the issue was how to visualise them and why this was important. What role could televisual animals play in realising the purpose and charter of the ABC? Which animals were best suited to the liberal humanist project of public broadcasting and how should they perform? How should animals be represented in order to generate pedagogic or entertaining or political effects? These questions drive the historical and empirical focus of this book, and we explore them through a series of case studies that are loosely chronological. However, we are less interested in detailed institutional changes in the ABC than in the shifting cultural techniques that crafted natural history animals and made them public and potent for audiences. To this end, we begin with an exploration of some early sightings of animals on Australian newsreel and cinema screens long before the arrival of television. These animals were public in the sense that they were visible and distributed across various communication networks, but they were not yet "public" in a governmental sense. They were not significantly burdened with collective concerns about animal realities or human-animal relations, nor were they expected to improve or educate populations. They were there to amuse and fascinate human observers but not to pose questions to them.

In its early years, ABC television nurtured a variety of new animals. Just like radio before it, televisual animals popped up in numerous programs manifesting all sorts of behaviours from cute and charismatic to anthropomorphic. However, it was with the development of the distinct format called "informational and documentary television" that the ABC began to identify the new medium's special appeal and capacity for visualising animals.[4] Almost as soon as it commenced broadcasting, ABC television screened nature programs imported from the BBC like the chat show *Look* (BBC, 1955-1968), which involved animal footage interspersed with interviews with wildlife cinematographers and naturalists. Gradually, the ABC began producing a scattering of locally made "nature films" in which animals were displayed and discussed as representative subjects of the natural world, a place that was promoted as both important and newly accessible thanks to the wonders of television. It was also a natural world that

---

4   Australian Broadcasting Commission, *Annual Report*, 1957, 25.

was to be increasingly framed through a settler-national lens as an "Australian nature", which ensnared televisual animals in relations of colonial power.

These early natural history animals rapidly became very popular and very influential. By the 1970s they had gained ascendancy over the many other animals roaming the screens of ABC TV and were identified as having a special role to play in educating and informing audiences. Hence the establishment of their own enclosure, the Natural History Unit, which was set up in 1973 to consolidate and co-ordinate the production of nature programs.[5] The animals captured and contained in this unit had a range of duties. They were expected to inform audiences about everything from the secrets of nature, to scientific facts, to threats to the environment, to national identity. The natural history animal was becoming a public servant, obliged to captivate and bind audiences to animals in certain ways and to generate various public effects and values.

This transition from the animal as entertainment to the animal as public object and public servant signals a range of political questions that inform our analysis. Paralleling our historical perspective is a more pressing concern with how natural history animals have been *made public* and the effects of this complex process. Our aim is to investigate how natural history animals emerged and how these creatures acquired the capacity to generate distinct forms of public interest and public value. In the case of the ABC, for example, how did they become implicated in the wider political rationalities of this broadcaster? Were they recruited to service the ABC Charter, enrolled to give expression to pre-constituted values and national culture? Or were they involved in helping to shape and define these terms by producing specific animal inflections for the categories "public" or "national" while simultaneously emerging as a remarkable new species?

Central to our argument is the assumption that these categories are unattached abstractions that are configured and given meaning through the generative effects of making and circulating media content. The issue is: How were animals implicated in this process? What sorts of animal performances were seen as best suited to creating public

---

5   Australian Broadcasting Commission, *Annual Report*, 1974, 32.

Introduction

interest or informing national audiences? What kinds of publicness did natural history animals generate and how were audiences invited to gather around them? And what positive effects were assumed to flow from watching them? In posing these questions, we are less concerned with the representational adequacies or excesses of natural history animals on TV than with how they were made into what Noortje Marres and Javier Lezaun describe as "devices of the public".[6]

By the 1980s, especially with the screening of the internationally celebrated series *Nature of Australia* (ABC, 1988), made for Australia's bicentenary, natural history animals on the ABC were celebrated for nurturing environmental awareness, supporting conservation, making previously inaccessible or disappearing species visible, communicating science and much more. The rise of the televisual natural history animal on the ABC was judged as *good* for audiences, *good* for the nation and *good* for the environment, but what about for the animals? How did their capture and containment by public broadcasters produce new realities for them? And what questions did these animals come to pose to us?

These questions drive this study. In pursuing them we want to trouble two familiar critiques of natural history animals on television and wildlife TV more widely. The first is a significant critique from the huge field known as media studies; the second is the lesser known but growing field of eco-media. Both these fields have devoted a lot of time to investigating the representational inadequacies and troubling effects of natural history animals. Across numerous studies, media analysts have exposed everything from the exploitative conditions of production central to these programs, to the excessive use of special effects and techniques of simulation, to the proliferation of spectacular purified natures that no longer exist. In this line of thinking, the nature and animals portrayed in natural history television are considered so fabricated, so removed from the reality of a degraded anthropogenic world, that they operate in the realm of pure fantasy.[7] Far from supporting "environmental awareness" and conservation, natural

---

6 Marres and Lezaun 2011, 489.
7 See, for example: Chris 2006; Cubitt 2005; Louson 2018; Mitman 2009; Pick and Narraway 2013 for a sample of these critiques.

history animals are accused of fuelling popular denial about the state of the planet. In a brutal review of David Attenborough's legacy, George Monbiot wrote in *The Guardian* newspaper that the television naturalist had created complacency, confusion and ignorance by refusing to show audiences the reality of serious ecological collapse and massive species decline.[8]

The second critique resonates with this but comes from philosophically inflected animal studies. Here, the "electric animal", as Akira Mizuka Lippit terms it,[9] is judged as a spectral effect of industrialisation. As animals were removed from the phenomenal world, they were displaced into the simulated and virtual worlds of zoos and cinema. In this process, they became available to humans as communication devices, as symbols of new structures of thought about nature and the superiority of the human subject. For Lippit, these technical animals are pale versions of their real selves, a lasting reminder of the destruction and disappearance of animals. They may now be abundant on screens, and humans may be comfortable being surrounded by them, but electric animals manifest a technical echo not a living voice.[10]

Both these critiques are rich and politically astute and signal significant trouble in the televisual Edens that natural history animals often inhabit. But they also have some serious limitations. In the rush to identify cultural and ideological effects, the mediated vitality and realities of these animals are often diminished. There is too much focus on representations rather than on how they are composed and accounted for, and how these textual animals acquire affective and political capacities. For us, the key issues are what has actually come to count as a "natural history animal" on ABC television and how these animals have been variously composed over time. More critically, we ask in what ways have these televisual creatures provoked new modes of knowing animals and new modes of becoming affected by them? What has been at stake, politically, in making animals visible and public in this particular way? What new forms of political attention *and*

---

8 Monbiot 2018.
9 Lippit 2000.
10 Lippit 2000, 21.

inattention about human–animal relations and plural worlds has the rise of the televisual natural history animal generated?

Approaching animals from this perspective reconfigures many of the concerns already swarming around screen animals and opens up a whole new set of issues. For a start, it challenges the idea that natural history animals on the ABC were merely surfaces on which existing ideologies and forms of power over animals were inscribed. Sometimes, this was definitely the case. There is no question that many natural history animals have carried a range of symbolic and representational burdens. They have been rendered passive objects of human curiosity, definitive representatives of their species, capable of revealing scientific facts and aesthetically spectacular. But they have been much more. To confine natural history animals within the framework of representation, and to deploy critique of these representations as the primary mode of analysis, is to erase the presence and potency of these mediated creatures. Of course, these are not embodied animals; they don't bite back.[11] They are composed and "factitious", but they are also often vital, compelling and affecting. They have a televisual life that is built up through everything from narrative, to camera points of view, to soundtracks, to the force of their being but also, most critically, in the interest and curiosity that comes from audiences watching them and being lured by their performances. As Vinciane Despret argues, showing an interest, feeling the pull of animals on the small screen that enchant or move or terrify us, is an opening out to being transformed, to caring.[12] Our claim is that many natural history animals have prompted audiences to view the world differently, to acknowledge multispecies plurality, even to become more ethically attuned or obligated to nonhuman others. This claim is not universal: the diversity of natural history animals and animal stories means that there is no singular "ABC natural history animal"; there are, instead, situated animals with differing capacities to pose questions and to be affecting.

---

11 Despret 2016.
12 Despret 2016, 130.

Approaching ABC animals: Mediation and mediatisation

How then to investigate these animals and to understand the ways in which they became televisual? Our experience in the ABC archives and watching hours of footage shows that making natural history animals was generally a complex and messy process involving myriad human skills and practices, technical apparatuses and cultural conventions. While this institutional media apparatus and ecology unquestionably shaped these animals to fit particular demands, it was never a top-down process of complete capture and containment. At the same time as animals were corralled into the public broadcasting environment and its constraints and conventions, they also pushed this environment into new configurations and provoked new communicative techniques. The origins of these natural history animals, then, were in the practices and *event* of wrangling them to become televisual and public. ABC animals were public in the literal sense that they circulated in accessible free-to-air networks and addressed different audiences. But they were also public in a more performative sense. These animals called publics into being; they generated new interest in animals – what they were, how they should be observed and why they mattered. Not only did ABC animals become implicated in enacting the governing logics of public service broadcasters (PSB), translating the rationalities of public broadcasting through their bodily performances, they also generated encounters with audiences in which new and different interactions between humans and animals were made possible.

In pursuing the changing practices and cultural techniques involved in making natural history animals on the ABC, we want to shift understandings of "making" from a predominant focus on media production practices to include a more ontological orientation. We are interested in how animals practically got to be on ABC TV and how they were *made real* in this context; how their performances depended on particular styles of reference that rendered them plausible in this setting. Our interest is in how natural history animal realities and worlds were composed in various sites and on various occasions within the ABC. We want to know what kinds of habits and manners of being these animals came to display on television and how these versions of animals were organised and framed. This ontological orientation assumes that animal realities on television are not self-evident; they have to be crafted and they have to be explained and accounted for.

Understanding animal modes of being or ontologies on television, then, is an empirical process focused on investigating the myriad practices that composed ABC animals and how these practices emerged and changed. What kinds of technologies, knowledges, visual techniques and conventions made animals televisual and justified them as the way natural history animals were meant to be? And how did animals, themselves, participate in or resist these framings? Which particular animals and animal qualities were privileged in the drive to render them televisual, and which were excluded? How did these animals perform and how did these performances configure the human viewer? How did public animals provoke new human dispositions, interests and concerns? For just as ABC television made animals public, it also made publics that learned to be affected by these animals in new and various ways.

The approach we develop in this book draws on three key theoretical inspirations: science and technology studies (STS), screen studies, and philosophically inflected animal studies that examine "animalities" or how animal worlds are created. The idea of animality disrupts reductive or mechanistic models of animal behaviour and investigates the diverse textures of animality – for example wild, domestic, technical or televisual – and their imbrication with the "human". This hybrid conceptual toolkit challenges many of the assumptions underpinning existing media studies of televisual animals, especially around issues of authenticity and fabrication. Within the very broad and conceptually diverse field known as "media studies" there has been growing interest in the rise of wildlife or natural history television as a genre and the unique characteristics of these screen animals. Beyond a focus on the historical evolution of the genre and its political economy within the global television industry,[13] there is also a rich body of work exploring the technical and creative practices involved in capturing and creating animal content for television.[14] Many of these studies document and critique the extensive use of

---

13 See Chris 2006; Cottle 2004; Mitman 2009.
14 See Bousé 2000; Gouyon 2016.

techniques such as reconstruction, staging and re-enactment, as well as the use of stock footage or imprinted or domesticated animals to simulate animal realities in the wild.[15] Then there is the post-production work of editing, narration, special effects and laying down soundtracks in order to create convincing and entertaining natural history animals.

While media studies accept these production techniques as structurally necessary to making animals that are suitably televisual, lurking between the lines is a lingering anxiety about the distorted or fabricated nature of TV animals. For Phil Bagust, "special effects" have become so fundamental to wildlife and natural history TV that the result is animals that are fantastically enhanced and largely simulated.[16] Derek Bousé echoes this point when he notes that wildlife media convey the natural world in terms set down by the medium *not* reality: "wildlife film and television depict nature close-up, speeded-up and set to music, with reality's most exciting moments highlighted and the 'boring' bits cut out".[17] At the heart of these observations is the implication that media representations of animals are never able to adequately capture the *pre*formed or authentic nature of animal being. The expectation that animals must instrumentally service the economic imperatives and cultural protocols of the format, that they be obediently and properly televisual, is seen as undermining any substantive commitment to actuality.[18] The cumulative effect of these critiques of media animals as "constructed" is that they are implicitly equated with the fake and *unreal*. This confirms Bruno Latour's observation about the fundamental problem with the idea of construction: "*either* something was real and not constructed, *or* it was constructed and artificial, contrived and invented, made up and false".[19]

The contrived and made-up nature of animals on the ABC is a given. The challenge is how to get beyond the real/unreal opposition and the moral anxieties this seems to generate about what "the media"

---

15   See Bagust 2008; Chris 2006; Mitman 2009.
16   Bagust 2008, 213.
17   Bousé 2000, 3.
18   Mitman 2009.
19   Latour 2005a, 90 (emphasis in original).

do to animals. Bousé describes this anxiety as "simulation and its discontents".[20] He argues that when investigating screen animals, the issue is not real versus unreal but how the relations between reality and realism are configured. Rather than yearn for a referent in the wild or critique these animals as fabrications, televisual animals need to be understood as creating their own fields of reference, their own accountability relations that establish what is plausible in this setting. The challenge, as Phil Bagust argues, is to understand the nature of these accountability relations and how they are generated in distinct media ecosystems.[21] For Bousé, techniques of media construction draw attention to the conventions of realism and meaning-making, *not* the unreal. The work of constructing a televisual animal involves the double process of signification: making something real and making sense of it at the same time.

This resonates with debates in STS about the making of realities. In this field, construction has acquired a militantly performative meaning and is akin to Bousé's account of realism as a "reality effect". John Law, for example, argues that constructing realities involves three interrelated processes: the making of particular realities, the making of particular statements about those realities, and the creation of inscription devices that produce those realities and statements.[22] Because realities are multiple and constantly in the making, and because they are not independent of the devices used to represent them, they are difficult to essentialise. Instead, the challenge is to investigate how particular entities or realities come to seem the way that they are, to analyse how they are done. Enacting or performing realities demands a focus on the practices and techniques involved, not with the aim of assessing their representational adequacy but with the goal of understanding which bodies, discourses, technologies, objects and so on are brought into relations to assemble this reality.

This theory of reality prompts a range of philosophical questions about the independence of an external or anterior reality, "out there". Two brief points can be made about this. First, the outside world is

---

20   Bousé 2000, 9.
21   Bagust 2008.
22   Law 2004, 31.

independent of us and in the process of enacting realities it pushes back and participates in how realities are done. Animal bodies and behaviours, for example, have significant force and agency in configuring the technical practices and inscription devices that are deployed to make them televisually real. As many histories of the evolution of wildlife television reveal, filming animals often involves significant technological innovation and ingenuity to accommodate their elusive, aggressive or strange activities. Second, this anterior animal reality is not necessarily pure or authentic or unmediated. As Latour[23] and Nick Couldry and Andreas Hepp[24] insist, we can never be outside of mediation. Anterior reality, as Law describes it, is: "a large hinterland of inscription devices and practices already in production".[25] The issue, then, is not where does an unmediated or real animal live but how does this particular animal reality come into being?

This STS or performative approach to reality makes it possible to investigate how natural history animals on television are enacted and their various reality effects. It also challenges the assumption that media observe and represent an unconfined fixed reality. Instead, the activity of television production has to be seen as a provocation or event that calls forth various animal realities. These realities are always partial and always crafted, and plenty of the world is excluded, neglected or othered. The critical point is that the idea of enacting or provoking reality begins from the assumption that natural history animals on the ABC had to be *done* rather than discovered.

Focusing on the ontologies that ABC natural history animals display and how these were assembled enables a shift from a representational idiom to a performative one.[26] Rather than critique the adequacy or accuracy of animal representations in relation to an authentic animal reality, we want to investigate *how* ABC animals emerged as contingent outcomes of numerous situated practices and devices; how these animal realities were mediated and composed; and their particular cultural effects and productivity. More critically, we

---

23 Latour 2005a.
24 Couldry and Hepp 2016.
25 Law 2004, 31.
26 Muniesa 2014, 10.

Introduction

want to know how they shaped new perceptions and ways of knowing animals. We are indebted to media studies investigations of animals on screen, but we want to put these into conversation with STS and its concerns with how the social is assembled. We see natural history animals on the ABC as unique "reality engines",[27] as creatures that make and mediate the social.

This approach assumes that media are thoroughly embedded in shaping everyday social worlds. As Couldry and Hepp point out: "material processes of mediation constitute much of the *stuff* of the social".[28] This shift from the media *and* society to the social *as* mediated opens up new lines of thinking about ABC animals. Firstly, it demands an investigation of the specific practices of mediation that were developed to communicate animals on television; a commitment to understanding the myriad relations and relays that were developed to attach animals to the project of public service broadcasting, to attach meanings to these animals, and to attach audiences to animals. What kinds of mediators transformed and translated animals so that they could comfortably inhabit a televisual environment and domestic living rooms? And how did these processes implicate humans in new social relations with them; how did they provoke new ways of experiencing animals?

Equally significant is an analysis of how this emerging species, "the natural history animal", was connected to wider changes that saw the increasing "mediatisation" of animals throughout the 20th century. Mediatisation is akin to Lippit's idea of the electric animal or the reappearance of animals in technological forms.[29] It led to many animals finding homes in new communication media, and to audiences that became utterly comfortable with encountering them in these settings, comfortable with the particular animal realities these media created. These audiences were at ease with the idea that screen animals were simply another mode of animal being and were open to being affected by them as a result.[30]

---

27   Haraway 2008.
28   Couldry and Hepp 2016, 3.
29   Lippit 2000.
30   Lorimer 2015, 120.

Mediatisation is distinct from mediation. It refers to those large-scale and proliferating infrastructures of communication that became central to constructing social realities over the 20th century.[31] The creation of PSBs is one important example of this transformation. These unique institutions were part of wider changes that incorporated media into everyday life and shaped popular and political cultures. Like all media, PSBs operate in clusters and associations with other communications systems to create aggregates of change and new social realities. So, when it comes to animals on the ABC, we have to consider how the particular mediations and ecologies of television worked in relation to other sites and media for making animals public such as zoos and museums, radio, cinema and newspapers. How were televisual animals connected to other infrastructures of communication that made animals public in the 20th century? And what kinds of changes in social reality did the widespread mediatisation of animals, particularly the rise and normalisation of the televisual animal, prompt? To pursue these questions, a dual focus is required. We need to develop an approach that is attentive to the specificities of how ABC animals were captured and how new realities for them were crafted in this unique broadcasting and governmental ecology. And we need to be attuned to how this species was part of wider transformations that saw the increasing mediatisation of animals and the emergence of new social perceptions and framings of them.

If ABC animals emerged from networks of mediation in this PSB, and were also evidence of wider patterns of mediatisation, how can we investigate these interrelated but distinct processes? What conceptual toolkit is necessary for this task that is *both* a historical study of how a media organisation made a new species of animal and an assessment of how mediatised animals circulated and came to influence wider "social figurations" or durable networks of meaning and communicative exchange between humans and animals?[32] By opening up a conversation between screen studies, STS and animal studies, we aim to develop a creative and politically incisive account of how ABC natural

---

31   Couldry and Hepp 2016, 35.
32   Couldry and Hepp 2016, 64.

history animals were realised and how they generated significant cultural and political effects.

As outlined, this approach diverges from critiques of wildlife TV that foreground concerns with the unreality of televisual animals and exploitative or ideological modes of vision. We also have concerns about the realities ABC animals inhabit, but they take a different form. We are interested in how these realities were assembled: What material chains and relays involving myriad processes linked animals to the screen and how were these realities framed and authorised? How were audiences and publics implicated in these relays and how did they provoke various intersubjective and political encounters? What kinds of relations were established between humans and animals in natural history programs? Did ABC animals invite audiences to *become with them* as companion species or *become alongside them* as distinct but connected; or *become sovereign to them*: human subjects happy to be educated or entertained by animal objects?[33] We want to open up a space for deliberation and political analysis that proceeds from concerns about what kinds of animal–human associations were provoked in this televisual environment and in wider social figurations that the ABC was connected to, such as, for example, colonial, national and ecological dynamics.

Capturing, provoking, inhabiting

How were ABC natural history animals crafted and what were the impacts of their public circulation? In order to pursue this question and its historical and political implications, this book is organised into three parts. These parts focus on key practices that were fundamental to realising a natural history animal: *capturing, provoking* and *inhabiting*. Each of these practices is technical and performative. They foreground the techniques and devices deployed to craft a natural history animal and their reality effects: how these practices made animals that were both credible and culturally durable. They also foreground the political dynamics implicated in making animals public and shifting

---

33   Haraway 2008.

human–animal relations. To capture or provoke animals is to implicitly privilege human control, whereas to inhabit has the possibility of exploring how we live in a common world with animals and share a common fate. While most of the chapters that follow focus on the ABC animal, some other examples have been selected to extend the analysis and highlight different forms of capture, provocation and inhabitation in related media.

In Part One we explore the practice of capturing animals for human observation in early Australian screen culture and the various forms of captivation this generated in audiences. Central here is the relationship between cages and cameras. Just at the moment when animals were disappearing from many natural and everyday settings, early screen media often deployed cages to contain animals and facilitate effective visual capture. The question is how did images of captured or hunted animals in newsreels and cinema provoke curiosity in audiences and shape distinct modes of interpretation and engagement? What human dispositions and affects did animal capture on screen provoke: superiority, curiosity, amusement? Chapter 1 explores two examples of pre-televisual capture that focus on endemic marsupials that are in the process of being eradicated from their milieu as it is encroached by settler agriculture. The first case explores the now iconic 1933 newsreel footage showing the last thylacine in Beaumaris Zoo pacing towards extinction in a desolate cage. The second examines *The Trail of the 'Roo*, a 1931 documentary about a kangaroo cull in the Riverina that also included capturing some live animals for urban exhibition. These examples prefigure the rise of the televisual animal in important ways. Not only do they highlight the technical necessity of containment in crafting various animal realities on screen, they also show different modes of publicness. These animals were public in the literal sense of being visible and in wide circulation, but they were not public in the more political sense of embodying various issues or collective identifications. They were objects of human fascination or entertainment, but their performances were not designed to educate audiences or provoke forms of public interest or concern. The thylacine might be almost extinct, the kangaroos might be terrified of capture, but these animal realities were not framed in ways that called concerned publics into being.

Introduction

With the invention of television, these capturing practices persisted. Chapter 2 explores some of the earliest wildlife TV shown on the ABC. David Attenborough's first TV show, *Zoo Quest* (BBC, 1956), went to air on Australian screens in 1960 and featured him on an expedition to the jungles of Borneo capturing orang-utans for the London Zoo. Cages play a critical role in this program and are central to making these animals visible, but there is also a sequence showing Attenborough tracking orang-utans through dense jungle and attempting to capture them on film "in the wild". In this sequence, the camera is not nearly as effective as the cage as a technology of capture. Orang-utans in remote treetops prove to be very elusive. *Dancing Orpheus* (ABC, 1962) is the second example explored. This landmark, award-winning documentary was one of the first "nature shows", as they were called, made by the ABC in 1962. It featured the superb lyrebird. Unlike *Zoo Quest*, *Dancing Orpheus* had no humans or cages visible on screen. While the program was narrated by an authoritative male voice, the lyrebird appears alone in a state of spontaneous self-betrayal performing its beautiful natural self. In *Dancing Orpheus*, making the lyrebird public involved various strategies of aestheticisation that positioned viewers as lucky witnesses to a natural performance that the wonders of television made possible. In both these examples, the animal can be considered as an engine of translatability for various public broadcasting imperatives. The logic of the visual capture and narration is predicated on the imperative of educating audiences rather than merely entertaining them. The lyrebird is valued as aesthetically and scientifically important and therefore worthy of televisual exhibition. The natural history animal was starting to take form.

Central to the analysis in Part One is the claim that devices for capturing and containing are not only structurally necessary to making animals public, they also have distinct performative and political effects. For Javier Lezaun and colleagues: "containment is to be understood in the sense of confinement or restraint but also as a holding … containment is close to the notion of a device which can convey an idea of storing, separating, delineating and allocating but also of articulating in discourse."[34] This account of containment

---

34 Lezaun, Muneisa and Vikkelsø 2013, 280.

recognises it as both a form of capture *and* a dynamic process for making realities. The containment device is not a neutral holder; it has effects and it configures what is contained in two senses: by delineating a boundary and separating things off from the world but also by framing and projecting them back into the world and capturing or orienting viewers to them. The effects of containment are not static, they are dynamic and generative.[35]

The natural history animal was an outcome of numerous containment processes, but it took a while to be configured within the ABC. In many existing accounts, these animals are assumed to be the product of the Natural History Unit (NHU) that was established in the early 1970s and closed down in 2007. However, this assumption belies the presence of animals across numerous departments in ABC TV long before and after the demise of this unit. It also obscures the complex processes whereby animals became contained and domesticated by the classification "natural history", which effectively marginalised other realities for them. Evidence from the NHU's early history shows that in the period before the classifications and cultural codes of the natural history genre had been fully established, there was not always a clear notion of *how* animals should be captured for TV, or how they might captivate viewers' interest; what televisual animals might be and how they should perform was uncertain. Codes, conventions and compelling ways of accounting for animals took time to be stabilised before animal performances on TV could be normalised and accepted as believable in this context, before the natural history animal could confidently inhabit television.

Part Two explores the processes whereby the actual material reality of animals becomes a televisual reality. The central concept driving the analysis is provoking or intervening to trigger an effect. Provocation challenges that idea that natural history television observes and represents an unconfined reality. Instead, the activity of television production has to be understood as an incitement, an event that calls forth various animal realities. These realities are always partial and always crafted, and plenty of the world is excluded, neglected or othered. The critical point is that the idea of enacting or provoking

---

35   Hawkins, Potter and Race 2015.

Introduction

reality assumes that ABC animals had to be composed and staged rather than found and documented. Rather than yearn for an unmediated or authentic animal, provocation foregrounds the myriad practices whereby a particular reality is enacted. Making animals public on television was an exercise in extensive and multiple relays of intervention, creativity and mediation – the issue is how were animals provoked and how were their performances authorised and accounted for as credible?

Our research in the ABC archives revealed innumerable technical and material interventions into animal worlds in order to make a natural history animal. In investigating these archives, there was no accounting for what you might find. Consider this random sample: extensive correspondence with a conservation biologist about how to safely fly a platypus from Tasmania to the ABC's Melbourne studio for a film shoot; an expenses claim from a cameraman who'd been living in remote Australia waiting – unsuccessfully – to film a rare bird; requests for a docile domesticated wombat that could stand in for a wild one and endure the rigours of filming. These examples offer rich insights into the complexities of composing a natural history animal: the vast material chains and relays involved in assembling its televisual reality and the ways in which the material reality of the animal had to be both negotiated and provoked. They also highlight the laborious processes of assemblage, the art of bringing about a reality suitable for television. In these processes the "real" animal, the referent behind the representation, was often an elusive element, confirming Michael Lynch's claim that "referential truth is not an essence that is transported from beginning to end; rather it is a contingent, certified, assessment".[36]

Chapters 3 and 4 explore the dynamics of provoking. In Chapter 3 the experiences of filmmakers, artists and scientists working on ABC natural history film shoots during the 1970s and 80s are analysed. Key documents investigated include the 1973 shooting diary of legendary Australian natural history cameraman, David Parer AO, when he was in the field filming the *Wildlife of Papua New Guinea* (ABC, 1975) series. Here we see how the natural history genre was practically crafted and materialised. We also examine reflections from scientists and

---

36 Lynch 2005, 37.

artists involved in making natural history programs about the challenges and frustrations of wrangling animals. These empirical materials reveal how animal worlds were intervened in, how animals pushed back or refused to co-operate, and how the provocations of TV production incited a reality rather than discovered it.

Chapter 4 examines the Sky TV series *David Attenborough's Conquest of the Skies* (Atlantic Productions, 2014), which screened on the ABC in 2015. The key focus is Episode 4, called "The Making of David Attenborough's Conquest of the Skies" (Colossus Productions, 2014). This behind-the-scenes episode supposedly "showing all" revealed the mess and contingency of wildlife production and also the agency of the animal body. It plays off the difference between the disciplined and objectified natural history animal that screened in the official series and the domesticated working animal that was actually used in the shoot and that was an unpredictable "talent": in this case, a whooper swan imprinted on a human trainer and incited to perform a scientific fact on cue, over and over again.

Finally, where did natural history animals live? In Part Three we examine the dynamics of inhabiting. Throughout the evolution of these animals, different locations have been privileged as their "home". These locations have a profound effect on how animals are represented. Modes of inhabitation shape not only animal habits but also how humans are positioned in relation to them. Are humans part of the same world or looking in on a separate wild, remote or disappearing reality? The most popular places animals have inhabited on the ABC are "nature", "the environment" and the nation. However, in late 2020 the "planet" entered the scene with some groundbreaking ABC programs on the fate of animals and ecologies in this time of climate change. Each of these sites displaced "the outback", one of the most popular locations prior to the rise of natural history animals. They also generated distinct animal modes of being and public concerns. "Nature" was very different from "the environment" and posed far fewer questions to audiences. It was often a purified and timeless space, whereas the environment recognised human actions and impacts and invited audiences to accept some level of responsibility for the fate of animals.

Chapter 5 explores the acclaimed natural history series, *Nature of Australia: A Portrait of the Island Continent* (ABC, 1988). Produced as

Introduction

part of the ABC's contribution to Australia's 1988 bicentenary, *Nature of Australia* made visual the geological and biological processes shaping the continent and the species that inhabited it. It did this in terms that were at once both *natural* and *national*. *Nature of Australia* framed the continent's geology and wildlife as always already national by weaving national time into the fabric of the continent's deep geological time. Equally significant was how this extraordinary crafting of national wildlife was deemed "safe" in the controversial year marking the advent of the continent's European colonisation by inserting First Nations perspectives into the final episodes. First Nations' opposition to the bicentenary events were significant during 1988 and signalled that the celebration was controversial and contested. *Nature of Australia* skirted around this controversy by acknowledging Indigenous relations to animals and land management, as well as the environmental impacts of white settlement. These acknowledgements were limited and carefully controlled in order to maintain the dominant focus in the series on nationing nature. Curiously mirroring the processes of colonisation that the bicentenary painfully highlighted, this mode of inhabiting was contingent on the subordination of other temporalities – of the evolutionary, of the geological, of the Indigenous – to national time.

In Chapter 6 the recent emergence of a planetary focus in natural history or factual television on the ABC is examined. After the Natural History Unit was disbanded in 2007, production of this type of content was generally outsourced to independent production companies. In December 2020 the ABC ran a themed series of programs titled "Your Planet". In various on-air and online promotions, the focus of the series was described as "the changing environment and solutions to climate change". Programs like *Big Weather: And How to Survive It* (Northern Pictures, 2020), *Wild Australia: After the Fires* (Northern Pictures, 2020) and *Reef Live* (Northern Pictures, 2020) all invoked a "sense of planet";[37] that is, a deterritorialisation of the links between culture, place and environment and a recognition of how humans, animals and habitats are mutually implicated in whole earth processes. What was so remarkable about these programs about planetary modes of inhabiting was how they evoked ethical effects that disrupted anthropocentrism

---

37 Heise, 2008.

and connected animal lives to human lives in ways that suggested *mutual* implication in forces beyond control.

Animals as devices of the public

The chapters that follow show how ABC natural history animals emerged out of various practices of capture, provocation and inhabitation. However, there is another practice that underpins all these – making these animals public. Investigating the dynamics of this practice and its effects is at the heart of this study. We want to understand how animals were authorised, exhibited and circulated by the ABC and how publics were called into being and gathered around them. Central to our analysis is the assumption that there are diverse publics and forms of publicness and various processes for constituting these. But how can we assess these processes and ascertain their political effects? What kinds of "publicness" did ABC animals realise? One approach would be to critically evaluate how effectively ABC animals represented the ABC Charter; to read these creatures as successful or unsuccessful expressions of public value, public interest or citizen engagement. The problem is that this assumes that public value or public interest are the fixed preconditions for making ABC animals, rather than the contingent outcome of how these animals were visualised and circulated. Or to put this another way: ABC animals didn't express pre-existing normative values for the ABC, they helped to constitute them. They helped make the fiction of "the public" real.[38] They provoked new forms of engagement in audiences who were often configured as citizens or publics through their pleasure and interest in watching animals on screen. This performative approach highlights the ways in which publicness was enacted discursively and practically. Just as animals had to be made real in the ABC, so too did their suitability and credibility as *public things* – as media objects suitable for realising the ABC's obligations as a public broadcaster, as things worthy of televisual exhibition.

---

38 Warner 2002, 15.

Introduction

While "public" may be inscribed in the legislative and institutional frameworks that justify the ABC, and while it informs the wider governmental rationalities of the organisation, our interest is in the ongoing processes and techniques of public-making. There is a governmental dimension to this in the sense that policies and entrenched institutional practices and conventions framed how ABC animals were shown: which animals and modes of visualisation were privileged and why. But there is also an experimental dimension to publicness and public-making, and this is what we are more interested in. Our archival research revealed numerous debates about how to capture and engage audiences who were the constant imaginary collective invoked in the dynamics of provoking animals. Which audiences will be incited by this animal content? How will their curiosity be aroused? How will they be captivated and invited to look? How will they be addressed? This fixation with audiences underpins most televisual production, but in the ABC the audience has the potential to be more than a demographic or ratings measure. It is also a site where various calculations about the nature of publicness – what counts as public value or public interest – emerge. Of course, there are numerous other sites, such as in the commissioning process or in the internal allocation of funds, where these calculations happen, but audiences are often privileged. Even so, audiences and publics are not equivalent or interchangeable. They are, however, related, and it is the way they become related and entangled, and how animals are implicated in this, that is of central interest here. The issue is: How did natural history animals make audiences into citizen-viewers capable of distinct modes of public engagement with their screen realities?

Some of the ways this happened in the ABC was through invocations of citizen interest or national identity or by making animals matters of concern. In these situations, viewers were invited to comport themselves as audiences *and* as publics; sharing common identifications or collective anxieties about animals and their habitats and fate. These particular versions of citizenship or national identity were mediated by the *form* of public engagement, by the way animal realities were accounted for and how these accounts provoked particular modes of viewing and orientations to animals; how they encouraged audiences to watch as a citizen, or as an Australian. These accountability relations implicated ABC animals in ontologies of governance. They made them engines of translatability between governmental discourses committed to educating, informing and entertaining populations and intimate domestic practices of watching in private homes. "Public" communication was made private through particular modes of address, accounts and animal performances that provoked certain conventions, hierarchies and exclusions. That made for very particular animal realities and animal–human interactions.

The types of publics and publicness generated in the ABC were diverse and constantly shifting. A significant focus in the chapters that follow is how shifts in publicness involved different engagements or contact zones with animals. In the early years of making animals televisual, the deficit model of the public was in evidence everywhere. This involved a mode of address and accounting for animals that presumed viewers knew little about them and needed to be educated. This pedagogic model configured the animal as an observable specimen and scientific object inviting citizen interest in its strange other world. Watching TV to *learn* was normalised as a distinct value and quality of the ABC–audience relationship. Animals realised this governmental relationship when they connected watching wildlife TV to becoming an informed citizen.

Numerous other genres of public-making were also in evidence. These ranged from engagements with animals as uniquely "Australian", as creatures who embodied and expressed the nation and invited national identifications, and, in more recent years, animals as public or political issues. The realisation of animal realities that provoked matters of concern, that posed questions to audiences about exploitation and abuse and species loss, is suggestive of "more-than-human" publics.[39] It also signals the escape of animals from the confines of the natural history genre with its limited codes and avoidance of too much controversy, and the emergence of animals as political objects *and* subjects. At the heart of our analysis is a focus on how different publics and modes of publicness are realised and how animals became shifting public and political beings in the history of the ABC.

---

39   Blue 2015.

Part One: Capturing

Animals have always been captured: trapped or incarcerated by humans for innumerable reasons. In this part we examine how animals were captured on early Australian cinema and television screens. Our focus in Chapter 1 is on some powerful examples from the 1930s of Australian animals filmed as they were pursued in hunting expeditions or caged after capture. The presence of the camera entailed another form of capture that involved turning these animals into moving images able to circulate and captivate audiences. In Chapter 2 the beginning of natural history television on the ABC during the 1950s and 1960s is examined. Hunting, capturing and caging animals feature in some of these early TV examples but this type of footage was rapidly displaced as the characteristics of the televisual natural history animal begin to take a shape. Ultimately, what came to matter for these animals was the absence of any visible sociotechnical devices of capture or other evidence of entrapment. Instead, the camera was sovereign, offering seemingly direct or unmediated access to animal modes of being in nature or what was soon to become known as "the environment".

Our aim is to investigate *how* these early, pre- and post-televisual, screen animals were captured and made visual. Equally critical is how these animals captivated audiences, for what is an image without a viewer; without an audience that is called into being and lured by the animals exhibited on screen? The value of investigating early or pre-televisual screen animals is that they offer important insights into the shifting interactions between modes of capture and modes of audience captivation and the political effects of these interactions. In many ways, the emergence of the natural history televisual animal was a significant rupture. Pre-televisual animals articulated very different modes of captivation than those that occurred with the development of public broadcasting and the growth of natural history television. These pre-televisual animals may have been captured and made public in the literal sense of exhibited to mass audiences, but they did not live in "the environment" and nor were they burdened with having to educate or improve audiences.

The examples we examine in Part One explore the interactions between capture and captivation in making animal realities on screen. While many of these examples document captured animals and the capturing or hunting of animals, in the sense of their physical restraint and confinement, film itself has also long been understood as a mechanism of capture – not of literally constraining bodies but of capturing particular moments in time, of capturing bodies in movement. The animal realities explored here are intensely mediated by both such devices of capture – the cage and the camera – that constrain animal bodies in space and arrest them from the flow of time. For cultural theorist Rey Chow, "capture is what activates reality, what makes reality happen".[1] Capture is the mechanism by which realities come to be both trapped and triggered. However, capture also has an affective dimension in its capacity to provoke "a state of emotive witnessing",[2] or what Chow terms "captivation": in her analysis, both capture and captivation are derived "from the imposition of power on bodies and the attachment of bodies to power".[3] Captivation evokes "the sense of being lured and held by means other than the purely physical, with an effect that is, nonetheless, lived and felt as embodied captivity".[4] Captivation in this sense of being held captive, of being bound to others in distinct ways, resonates with Jamie Lorimer's

---

1 Chow 2012, 166.
2 Lezaun, Muniesa and Vikkelsø 2013, 12.
3 Chow 2012, 6.
4 Chow 2012, 48.

discussion of the cultural techniques of wildlife media.⁵ These techniques implicate spectators in particular strategies that act on their affective responses. In doing so, they generate, as Lorimer continues, an "embodied disposition that establishes a habituated set of practices and feelings ... through which a person is oriented and makes sense of an encounter with human and nonhuman others".⁶

Such strategies of capture and captivation have been enduringly tied to assemblages of discourse, technologies and institutions which Tony Bennett has termed the "exhibitionary complex".⁷ For Bennett, the emergence of this complex was contingent on the rise of the natural sciences, the invention of photography and film, the art of taxidermy and the diorama, together with the proliferation of their associated public institutions – the cinema, the zoological garden and the natural history museum. It was over the late 19th and early 20th centuries that these institutions of exhibition not only came to increasingly share common "presentational configurations" through which animals were publicly displayed,⁸ they also shared in a *dispositif* of animal capture implicated in "the anthropological machine", which worked to adjudicate on the (indistinct) boundary between the human and nonhuman animal.⁹ In so doing, the exhibitionary complex shared in techniques that solicited, or sought to activate, a particular disposition in their audiences – an ontological-political disposition that proceeded in the assurance of the human as sovereign. Discursively and physically contained by this complex as "the animal", these nonhuman others come to be, as Melissa Boyde puts it, enduringly pressed into the "service of human subjectivity".¹⁰

The questions driving our analysis are: What was the role of cages, cameras and other forms of technical and cultural capture in visualising early moving-image animals just at the moment when they were disappearing from other natural settings? How did the logics of

---

5   Lorimer 2015.
6   Lorimer 2015, 122.
7   Bennett 1995.
8   Haraway 1992, chapter 3; Nessel 2012, 46.
9   Agamben 2004.
10 Boyde 2006, 1.

exhibition in zoos and cinema depend on captivating audiences and shaping how they looked at animals? What dispositions and affects did these early visual animals solicit in audiences? How were these viewer dispositions reconfigured with the rise of the natural history televisual animal? And how did these animals captivate audiences and generate distinct modes of looking and learning to be affected?

1
Cages and cameras
Screen animals before television

In 1933 the last thylacine captured in Tasmania was filmed pacing towards extinction in Beaumaris Zoo, Hobart. Two years earlier a short film, *The Trail of the 'Roo* (MCD Productions, 1931), documented a kangaroo hunt in the Riverina region of New South Wales. These kangaroos were being captured for exhibition in cities. Both these examples can be considered as Antipodean contributions to the tradition of "zoo films" and "hunt films" that, by the turn of the 20th century, were recognised as a global phenomenon.[1] Zoo films were evidence of an early cinematic practice that exploited the containment of animals.[2] Filming animals in a zoo was, as Jan-Christopher Horak puts it, "much easier and more convenient than chasing them in the wilds with a camera" – especially before the adoption of the telephoto lens.[3] To document their caged subjects, zoo films routinely enrolled the expertise of zookeepers and zoologists, the latter often doubling as filmmakers.[4] However, the purpose of these films was usually more

---

1 Horak 2006, 462.
2 Lawrence and Lury 2016, v.
3 Horak 2006, 462.
4 There was a close interconnection of expertise, technologies, institutions and personnel in the ways zoological and ethnographic subjects were made public in spectacles of colonial power: be it the display of humans in zoological gardens as in the well-known case of Ota Benga, the Congolese teen exhibited

about the distribution of exotic and spectacular animal images to entertain cinema audiences unable to attend urban zoos, than the production of material of scientific or pedagogical value. Exemplary here were the early films of the Lumière brothers shot at the London Zoological Garden in 1895.

Relying largely on the spectacle of the exotic animal's presence, zoo films suffered from a lack of action and narrative drive. The filming of hunted animals subsequently emerged as a popular genre for audiences seeking more excitement than the relatively static zoo film offered. The hunt provided a ready-to-hand narrative to structure the action: the stalk, the find, the kill. It also sanctioned a certain pleasure in violence towards animals. Hunt films were sometimes associated with scientific expeditions and museum fieldwork activities. A key example was *Roosevelt in Africa* (Pathé Frères, 1910), which documented Teddy Roosevelt's safari exploits and involved the collection of thousands of "skins" for the taxidermist's art, some of which were displayed in the hyperreal dioramas of the American Museum of Natural History.[5] Zoo and hunt films involved distinct modes of animal capture and display that were incorporated into the exhibitionary complex.[6] What was most significant about zoo and hunt films was the way in which they enrolled human and animal bodies in cinematic performances of animal vanishing. These films captured processes of animal (dis)appearance that, for many commentators, characterise the rise of the modern cinematic animal.[7] The "double movement of animal (dis)appearance" has been a defining trope of the critical literature on the exhibition of animals in zoos and cinema.[8] This movement rests on the paradox that modern technologies of vision and exhibition spectacularly increased the visibility of animals, at the same time as they were dramatically vanishing from the wild and receding from everyday life. John Berger

---

at the Bronx Zoo in 1906; or the ethnographic villages or "human zoos" popular at international exhibitions over the late 19th and early 20th centuries.
5   Haraway 1992.
6   Bennett 1995.
7   Berger 2009; Lippit 2000.
8   McMahon and Lawrence 2015, 9.

is the most influential critic to develop this paradox.[9] For Berger, the proliferation of animal representations coincided with the advent of a modernity that not only increasingly encroached on wildlife but also displaced agrarian populations, dislodging the everyday animal–human relations of rural life. In this context, Berger contends: "Public zoos came into existence at the beginning of the period which was to see the disappearance of animals."[10] Zoo animals, he continues, "constitute the living monument to their own disappearance".[11]

Elaborating on this proposition, media theorist Akira Mizuta Lippit argues:

> In its specular, zoological world, the modern animal evolved into a lost object that could then, in turn, be mourned. A new breed of animals now surround[ed] the human populace – a genus of vanishing animals, whose very being [was] constituted by that state of disappearing.[12]

These vanishing animals had an affinity with the new recording technologies increasingly associated with the moving image, and it is through these technologies that animals "found a proper habitat or world" on the screen.[13] Lippit continues: "The capacities of the technological media in general and the photographic media in particular to record and recall served as a mnemonic supplement that allowed modern culture to preserve animals".[14] If zoos and cinema provided monuments to the disappearance of animals and sites for memorialising their loss, cinema, in particular for Lippit, supplied the key emerging habitat for this new genus of spectral beasts.[15] However,

---

9   Berger 2009.
10 Berger 2009, 30.
11 Berger 2009, 36. Berger's account, originally published as an essay in 1977, has been contentious. See Burt (2002) in particular for a sustained critical engagement.
12 Lippit 2000, 3.
13 Lippit 2000, 25.
14 Lippit 2000, 25.
15 However, the close development of nature films and the natural dioramas have been famously documented in Haraway's (1992, chapter 3) account of

in identifying this new type, Lippit departs from Berger's argument. Lippit posits the double movement of animal (dis)appearance less as an effect of the paradoxical shifting relations between representation and referent under the conditions of industrial capitalism. Rather, this movement was constitutive of a new mode of being – one contingent on modern technologies of vision. It was in the flickering milieu of the modern screen that vanishing animals came to be reinvented as spectral creatures.

We are indebted to Lippit's argument about how animals came to inhabit the modern screen and the wider cultural processes that saw the emergence of spectral animals.[16] However, a focus on the spectral realities of screen animals can ignore the disposable animal body on which animal film has also often been dependent. As Rosemary-Claire Collard forcefully argues, "film's affective potential to electrify, animate or enliven has existed in tension with its reliance on an encounterable, killable and invade-able animal life".[17] This claim is particularly relevant to the two films we explore here. Both these films – David Fleay's footage of a thylacine at the Beaumaris Zoo (1933) and the McDonagh sisters' 1931 documentary featurette *The Trail of the 'Roo* – capture animal bodies that were considered disposable to the logic of settler colonialism and the expanding frontier of pastoral capitalism: a carnivorous marsupial believed to prey on livestock and herbivorous marsupials that competed with livestock for pasture. Both thylacines and kangaroos were targets of settler programs of extermination. The films analysed here are inseparable from that history.

---

the work of Carl Akeley. Akeley produced the hyperreal dioramas of the African Hall, American Museum of Natural History, New York, in which animals were presented in frozen motion as if captured by a still camera. Akeley invented the motion camera, which he developed in the research and preparation of these dioramas.

16   Lippit 2000.
17   Collard 2016, 472.

1 Cages and cameras

Marsupial capture/spectral beasts

Late in 1933 the Australian zoologist and naturalist, David Fleay, filmed an adult male thylacine at the Beaumaris Zoo, Hobart.[18] The film was shot a few months after the animal was captured in the Florentine Valley in southern Tasmania. This famous footage shows the muscular marsupial pacing about its bare enclosure. It yawns, demonstrating its massive gape, sniffs the air, scratches itself, lies down, before getting to its feet as if startled and starting to pace again. Without sound and with minimal editing, the footage lasts for 45 seconds.

Over the intervening years this vision has acquired historical significance as the first to capture the last of a species on celluloid.[19] Writing in 1986, the year the species was officially declared extinct by the Tasmanian government, and half a century after he filmed the Beaumaris Zoo's thylacine, Fleay recalled the experience: "Not long captured and still wearing the springer snare band about his right hind leg, this long, lean, softly padding animal had an ethereal appearance".[20] In writing of its ethereal qualities, Fleay proceeded in the knowledge that the animal's image represented a species whose time had all but officially expired. In this observation, he shared with his readers his sense that the thylacine that paced before his camera lens was somehow already a ghost. As he put it, the animal "was extremely delicate and light in a way that seems not to be of this world".[21] Carrying the impossible weight of being the last living representative of an extinct population, the "softly padding animal" could only walk among the undead. Fleay writes as if this zoo exhibit, as the last living trace of

---

18   To view this footage see: http://tinyurl.com/2s44ssbc. The gender of the captive animal has been in dispute and it was historically thought to have been a female. Museum zoologist Stephen Sleightholme (2011), in a close reading of the Fleay footage, has confirmed that the animal was in fact male.
19   In subsequent years Fleay, among others, staged an expedition (1945–46) in search of other specimens but to no avail. At the time he shot his footage, the once persecuted species had likely already all but disappeared from its range (see Paddle 2000).
20   Cited in Sleightholme and Campbell 2015, 285.
21   The empirical details used in these paragraphs are drawn from Guiler 1986; Paddle 2000; Sleightholme 2011; and Sleightholme and Campbell 2015.

a species, was fading before the camera. Here, it seems that the materialities of the zoo exhibit and the filmed animal were collapsing into a single ghostly presence that captured the poignancy of the historical moment: the recording of a species on the cusp of extinction.

Nevertheless, the thylacine's reality as spectral was as much to do with the ontology of the apparatuses that contained it as it was with the existential predicament of the animal as the last of its species. As Lippit has argued, with the emergence of modern technological media, animals "enter a new economy of being" – they come to "exist in a state of *perpetual vanishing* ... linger[ing] in the world *undead*".[22] In her reading of Bazin and Barthes' accounts of the photographic image, Laura Mulvey elaborates on the filmic undead.[23] The reality of the photographic image, she contends, is born of the paradox between the index and the uncanny: the index is an objective "incontrovertible fact, a material trace that can be left without human intervention, [it] is a property of the camera machine and the chemical impact of light on film".[24] The uncanny concerns the subjective experience of dis-ease, of unsettlement, that is "aroused by confusion between the animate and the inanimate, most particularly ... associated with death and the return of the dead".[25] For Mulvey, it is the photographic image's capacity to suspend time, to conflate life and death and blur the distinction between the animate and the inanimate, that generates "a sense of disquiet that is aggravated rather than calmed by the photograph's mechanical, chemical and indifferent nature".[26] In this sense, the photographic image is hauntingly produced in the intertwining of the index and the uncanny. The photographic image provokes an affective dissonance in its viewer through which its reality – a merging of the indexical and the uncanny – unfolds. In this sense, the photographic image is a mode of both capture and captivation: trapping the likeness of its animal objects and triggering the haunting of its human subjects.

---

22 Lippit 2000, 1 (emphasis in original).
23 Mulvey 2006.
24 Mulvey 2006, 55.
25 Mulvey 2006, 60.
26 Mulvey 2006, 61.

1 Cages and cameras

The ethereal presence that Fleay attributed to the Beaumaris thylacine is a central element of the reality provoked by his footage. It rests on the pathos of the representational burden of this thylacine as the last of its kind. However, it is also connected to the quality of film as index, as photochemical trace of what must have been. Fleay's film is testimony to the light that once played on the thylacine's coat that served to burn the animal's likeness on the film-stock. And yet there is a fragility, a vulnerability to such filmic insistence. The cinematic moment of capture is simultaneously the moment the referent disappears. The ontology of film is inescapably one of loss, of disappearance, of death. The slipperiness between sign and referent that the indexicality of film would seem to resolve with the materiality of the photochemical trace reasserts itself in the presence of a referent always on the cusp of vanishing. What is lost is the referent in this moment of registration. What is provocatively contained is the spectre of the last thylacine: an uncanny presence that is at once bounded and separated from the world, contained within the lightness of its cinematic being; and, framed and projected back into the world in its ethereal image, captivating viewers with the weight of species lost. It is a strange filmic intensity in which viewers, as Belinda Smaill contends, "constantly grapple with the play of absence and presence".[27]

This particular cinematic capture, however, is contingent on another device of containment – the cage, which is clearly visible in its grim austerity in Fleay's footage. The logic of the zoo exhibition is not strictly indexical. In its corporeal form, the animal is powerfully present but remains ontologically precarious – not in this case as a photochemical trace, but rather as a zoological remainder torn from its milieu and isolated in its enclosure. The pathos of the zoo animal is not that of the uncanny born of the temporal disjuncture of the mechanical image. Rather, it is the unsettlement produced by a spatial displacement maintained by the cage, by a nagging sense that the animal should be elsewhere, that it is literally not at home, but belongs to some indeterminable elsewhere out there "in the wild" to which its return is impossible. Contained in its bare isolation, the Beaumaris Zoo's thylacine was to stage a singular performance: representing its species

---

27   Smaill 2015, 150.

ex situ by becoming a specimen. As a zoo exhibit, the thylacine is a zoological remainder that insists, like the cinematic trace, on what must have been. The caged animal served as a diminished vestige of the wild lives (once) lived elsewhere. And, like the photochemical trace, the zoo remnant shares in the logic of animal disappearance, activating a disposition of pathos, of loss in those that the spectral animal both hails and haunts. Reduced to a tragic harmless trace of what once was elsewhere, the Beaumaris Zoo's thylacine becomes a monument by which to mourn the species' passing.

However, the affinities in these realities of disappearance that condition the precarious ontologies of the Beaumaris thylacine are disrupted in the moment of actual filming. To capture the animal on film involves entering the container that encloses it as a zoo exhibit. And, with this action, the experience of the animal transforms from the affectively powerful but physically harmless trace of the "once was" to a very lively agent of the present. As Catherine Simpson puts it: "As he paces his cage, the ghostly anguished presence of the soon-to-be-extinct [thylacine] … belies the animal's status as a predatory carnivorous marsupial."[28] Given the interval between Fleay's account cited above and the shooting of the footage, the ethereal qualities Fleay attributed to the Beaumaris Zoo's thylacine were more the effect of his encounter with his own film than with the thylacine itself as it paced before his lens. The brute reality of the zoo exhibit was of an altogether different order from its celluloid likeness. The earlier encounter was no doubt motivated by a desire to realise the potential of the camera as a scientific device for recording the real, and so generate a lasting document of what was increasingly recognised as a very rare specimen. Nevertheless, it was an encounter whose intensities were as far from cool scientific objectivity as they were from the chill of the ethereal. By all accounts, the encounter ran hot.

It is easy to imagine that when Fleay and the zoo's head keeper, Arthur Reid, entered the enclosure to film and photograph the thylacine, the adrenaline of the men and the marsupial was surging. The thylacine was visibly stressed by the presence of the two men with their unwieldy camera gear in its enclosure. The animal's wide gape captured

---

28   Simpson 2010, 50.

on the film footage is testimony to its displeasure. Prudently, Fleay and Reid had come prepared in the event of their captive's aggression. However, Fleay was not to leave unscathed. Reporting on the encounter, Fleay would write: "The big fellow in the zoo was not a safe companion inside his enclosure, and while photographs were being taken Mr Reid had to ward him off continually with a paling."[29] Reid's efforts to defend the naturalist as he worked beneath the curtain of his camera were not a total success. Following two warning "yawns", the animal broke Reid's defences and Fleay was bitten. And with the clamping of its large jaws, the full force of the thylacine's resistance bore down on the zoologist's buttocks. The injuries, it turned out, were superficial. Nevertheless, the attack was to leave Fleay with a scar – a further indexical record of the (career-making) encounter. It was later reported that Fleay wore this cicatrix as a mark of distinction – though on what occasions he revealed it go unremarked. The wound nevertheless endowed him with a form of corporeal capital that added to his accumulating zoological capital, to which the Beaumaris Zoo film was to prove a lasting contribution.[30]

Triggering and trapping the unsettling reality of "the last Tasmanian tiger", Fleay's footage articulates the ways in which early screen animals came to be provoked through various devices and techniques of capture. It also encapsulates the ways in which the affective logic of (dis)appearance that the film solicits – of a captivation by the ghostly, by the uncanny – is inescapably contingent on the disposability of the animal's body. Three years after Fleay filmed his footage, Benjamin, as the doomed thylacine was popularly known, was dead. Locked out of his shelter overnight, the animal died of exposure. With the zoo unable to afford adequate staffing, the neglected marsupial had become a casualty of the Depression, perishing on a cold September evening in 1936. Benjamin's corpse was taken to the Hobart Museum. The museum declared the thylacine's skin to be in too poor condition to warrant preservation and his body was abandoned on a municipal rubbish dump to decay among the city's refuse.

---

29 Cited in Sleightholme 2011, 953.
30 Fleay's other great zoological achievement was in 1943 with the first successful captive breeding of platypus in Healesville, Victoria.

The Trail of the 'Roo

The Trail of the 'Roo[31] was an early documentary featurette and "talkie" made by the McDonagh sisters, key figures in Australia's early motion picture industry.[32] One of several short documentaries they produced with Standardtone Sound Recording Studios, an early specialist in sound films, the featurette documented a kangaroo hunt in the Riverina region of New South Wales. Promotional material described the film in prosaic terms: "an interesting film showing how the kangaroo is hunted, captured and transported to the city for show purposes".[33]

The vision shows scenes in which panic-stricken animals are driven en masse down a narrowing race, where it was reported 60 persons and 30 motorcars took part in the drive.[34] Footage includes men with the corralled 'roos – one animal is kicked, another is restrained and paraded before the camera. The captured animals are subjected to a selection process. A number are shot and skinned for museum collections. Others are dragged by their tails and packed live into wooden crates destined for zoos.[35] Juxtaposed to the explicit violence of these scenes, subsequent sequences take a tranquil turn, focusing on a group of 'roos in an urban zoological garden.

The voice-over that accompanies the footage was scripted (though not spoken) by poet and journalist, Kenneth Slessor.[36] This informal commentary is a curious mix of light-hearted humour, with ceaseless hopping puns, and an anthropomorphising of the 'roos that unequivocally acknowledges their anguish: the 'roos are variously

---

31   Paulette McDonagh (Dir.) (1931) *The Trail of the 'Roo*. MCD Productions. A clip from this film can be viewed at: http://aso.gov.au/titles/documentaries/the-trail-of-the-roo/.
32   Cook 2015.
33   *The Trail of the 'Roo. Advertiser* 6 January 1933, 2. Screening in the country's capital cities in 1933, *The Trail of the 'Roo* was included in the newsreels distributed by Cinesound and Fox news services, where it was featured in a daily program.
34   On The Trail of the 'Roo. *Sun* 9 April 1926, 11.
35   It was stated that 70 'roos were taken to the Melbourne Zoo and another 45 to the zoo in Sydney (*Sun* 9 April 1926, 11). Presumably it was from these centres that the animals were exported to foreign zoos.
36   O'Regan and Walmsley-Evans 2016.

1 Cages and cameras

described as "victims" (after being skinned in the name of science) and as "chaps" and "prisoners" (when put into crates for transportation). In ascribing to the animals' subject positions that slip between the ordinary ("chaps"), the captive ("prisoners") and the suffering ("victims"), the voice-over opens the possibility of audience sympathy with the animals' pain. It is, however, an emotive recognition that is always disrupted by the next hopping gag. In this there is an unsettling doubling performed by the voice-over, which is at once a humorous making light of the footage while also acknowledging the injury portrayed. The narrative takes the viewer some way towards an affinity with the animals' predicament, only to pull back from it with the repetition of levity. The voice-over performs an ambivalent mode of audience captivation – oscillating between sympathy, and with it an implicit ethical recognition of 'roo suffering, and humour and ridicule denigrating the animals.

Interestingly, it appears the 1933 screening was not the first time that the footage was exhibited. A silent captioned film, *On the Trail of the 'Roo*, was released by Hellmrich Conrad and screened in Sydney and Melbourne between 1926 and 1927. According to newspaper reports, this film recorded a 'roo hunt shot in the same locations as the 1931 film, Widgiewa and Lake Cowal Stations. These articles also detail a number of scenes that are shared with the 1931 film.[37] Following the advent of sound technology, it appears likely this footage was repurposed by Standardtone and released as a "talkie".

Significantly, when this footage was first screened in 1927 it caused controversy over scenes of animal cruelty. The *Argus* reported:

> It is claimed that scenes involving distressing cruelty to kangaroos mar what is otherwise an interesting and entertaining production ... Certainly a picture of this nature would not be calculated to encourage a love for animals among those who witness ... the terrified animals [as they] are corralled in an area enclosed with wire netting. Here they are to be seen rushing blindly at fences in their efforts to escape their pursuers. Kangaroos maimed by rifleshot and stricken with pain and terror make a pitiful sight ...

---

37   See On the Trail of the 'Roo. *Sydney Morning Herald* 9 April 1926, 7.

Subsequently the animals are herded into a smaller pen, where they continue to be harassed, and further unedifying scenes are witnessed.[38]

These objections saw the film modified, with a scene cut where several kangaroos were shot. To the consternation of the film's defenders, the controversy also demonstrated the provocative power of the caption titles. One writer to the editor sought to explain that some content to which there were objections was not actually part of the vision, but rather alluded to by captions: "Complaint is made about kangaroos being shown throwing their 'joeys' away and being shot. There was never such a scene ... but there is a sub-title to th[is] effect".[39] In association with the vision of the distress of the drive and the carnage of the cull, the caption indicated, for some, an animal reality that exceeded what was actually screened. The caption alluded to a possible off-screen reality of unspeakable cruelty – female 'roos abandoning their young in terror, only to be shot.

The repurposing of the footage as a "talkie" responded to this controversy. The film's producers not only tried to lighten up the footage as entertainment, they also tried to make it more edifying by generating sympathy for the 'roos.[40] In this vein, the framing of the closing scenes at the zoological gardens served as a redemption of the violence that the 'roos have endured in their preparation for the exhibitionary complex. The voice-over credited the kangaroos' relocation to the zoo as a form of embourgeoisement: "shanghaied and taken far from home ... they become the centre of admiring crowds. No more bounding about the plains ... but the life of steady respectable suburban comfort." The horrors and injustices of the bush were thus

---

38 Kangaroo drive. Objections to film. Scenes suggesting cruelty. *Argus* 18 October 1927, 17.
39 Kangaroo film: To the Editor of The Argus. *Argus* 5 November 1927, 29.
40 As one columnist noted at the time that the footage was first screened, this was sympathy that the captioned footage did not seek, though it did solicit sympathy from some viewers, as the ensuing controversy attests. Kangaroo drive. Objections to film. Scenes suggesting cruelty. *Argus* 18 October 1927, 17.

redeemed by a charmed life in city zoos in Parkville, Melbourne, or Sydney's Mosman.

In documenting the act of collection, of the gathering of those that are to become zoological specimens, the film offers a forthright optic on the violence of these collecting practices. *The Trail of the 'Roo*, however, was no exposé in the contemporary sense designed to provoke moral outrage, uncovering the violence of making the zoological exhibit, of revealing what is concealed in the practices of making animals public. The hunting, the maltreatment, the death, were still largely spectacle. They were not offered as a source of moral indignation but as entertainment.

However, what is interesting about this film is the sense in which it is a behind-the-scenes foray into how a zoological specimen is made, how the animal begins to be formatted as a zoological exhibit. These scenes offer no particular insight into the animal's way of life. These scenes do not take the viewer into the lives of animal others. They are not invitations into the *umwelt*, into the sensory world of the 'roo. Rather, the film documents the formatting of the animal's body in preparation for exhibition while itself being complicit in that apparatus. In this, the scenes are exercises in the animal's negation as it is prepared for its display ex situ, as it is readied for its second life as public exhibit – as trace, as remainder, as remnant. The film is not only testimony to the disappearance of wildlife as the 'roos are deleted from the landscape: "No more bounding about the plains" was not just the fate of individuals captured for display, it was rural policy in New South Wales directed at kangaroo populations. The film is also an active agent in the 'roos' emergence as *the undead* of the exhibitionary complex.

In this connection, the performance of the corporeality of the animal is particularly significant. What the film documents is the processing of the animal body as it is rendered a zoological specimen, as it is corralled into a race for selection, skinned in preparation for the museum's taxidermy, or packed in crates in anticipation of the zoo's exhibition. These performances of the animal's body as provoked by the camera – dead and flayed, alive and caged – become exercises in a cinematic biopolitics: a provoked reality that enacts the bare life of that which is becoming a zoological specimen. The language of victimhood and suffering, of the prisoner, of the captured, no doubt signals the 'roos' enrolment in a carceral archipelago in which their selection for execution or for imprisonment finds their corporeality directed to the various institutions of exhibition – to the museum as preserved remains or to the zoo as living remainder, or to the cinema as photographic trace. The cinematic apparatus, in making a spectacle of the processing of the 'roos' bodies as they circulate from the field to centres of calculation and collection, the zoo and the museum, foreshadows the animal's body as valued not only as zoological specimen but also as public entertainment. In so presenting the animal's body, the veracity of its zoological worth becomes the currency of its value as spectacle.

This is demonstrated in several scenes that format the 'roo body as zoological exhibit, provoking an animal reality always on the edge of disappearance, always on the cusp of vanishing. In the first of these scenes, a kangaroo is wrestled to be paraded before the camera, restrained with a man either side holding a front limb, a hat placed atop the 'roo's head. At once anthropomorphised and humiliated by the hat, the animal's status as wildlife is diminished to a prop for human amusement. And in so doing, the scene establishes the animal's body as a body to be done to – a disposable body: a body to be abducted, to be destroyed, to be disappeared from the landscape – on which subsequent scenes make good. In a later scene, hunters gather around a hide hanging from a tree. Dismembered and flayed, the 'roo's body is disaggregated in anticipation of its preparation as museum specimen. The animal is destroyed so that its pelt might have a second life as a museum exhibit. In the final scene, a 'roo in the zoo is hand-fed by a man in a suit, ostensibly a scene of benevolent domestication and a counterpoint to the brutality and humiliation the animals endured as they were hunted and harassed. In contrast to earlier scenes, it offers an apparent moment of interspecies reconciliation; a rapprochement achieved cinematically by the tentative acceptance of food by the captive 'roo, but one that nevertheless continues human mastery over the 'roo's body. This is a body singled out not for destruction but for domination in a regime of care through which the 'roo is becoming a zoo exhibit.

There is no pretence of the camera as objective observer in these scenes. In the presence of the camera something must be done. The presence of the camera explicitly provoked these performances. They are actions performed for it, performed for the assumed amusement of imagined viewers. And, in doing so, they enact a provocation in which the animal's body is captured and contained so that it might disappear; so that it might be reformatted to become other than itself – as photographic trace, as corporeal remanent, as zoo exhibit or remainder. These scenes share in the activation of the kangaroo's body as a zoological specimen for exhibition. In this way, *The Trail of the 'Roo* draws together elements of early "zoo films" and "hunt films", with the passivity of the closely-observed zoo animal now provided a redemptive narrative and closure to the violence of the hunt.

Conclusion

As testimonies to cinema's spectral beasts, Fleay's footage of the Beaumaris Zoo's thylacine and the McDonaghs' *The Trail of the 'Roo* (MCD Productions, 1931) exemplify, in different ways, the techniques of capture/ captivation through which animals come to inhabit film in a perpetual play of absence and presence. While both films articulate a double movement of animal (dis)appearance, these marsupial performances of the cinematic undead are located in different regimes of value. The singularity of Fleay's thylacine presents an economy of excruciating scarcity, while the McDonaghs' multitude of 'roos represent an abundance to be suppressed. This differentiated economy of spectral beasts is consequential for the affective logics that come to captivate viewers. Fleay's footage draws out the affinity between the ontology of cinema and extinction in the melancholy of loss, which is captured by the photochemical trace of the animal's body: this passing moment, this passing species that will never be captured again. The McDonaghs' film highlights the agency of the camera in provoking the reformatting of the animal's body so it might have an afterlife as spectacle. Sympathy for the suffering of the vanishing body is retrofitted in audio form, ameliorating the violence of the mediation of 'roo as wildlife and its exhibitionary afterlife. Loss and sympathy serve as devices of capture/captivation, hailing and haunting spectators in cinematic performances of animal vanishing.

However, it is important to signal a specificity to these examples of animal (dis)appearance. They are informed by a cultural logic that diverges from the social disembedding of industrial capitalism that informs Berger's account of the memorialising of animal loss. These are presentations of marsupial vanishing, of forms of animal life endemic to south-eastern Australia, which have been displaced by the logic of settler colonialism and the demands of the pastoral economy. In this sense, these films capture the marsupial spectres that haunted the road of national progress. However, while the marsupial bodies here are those of scientific curiosity and entertainment, the films discussed above are not about "wildlife" or natural history animals as they would come to be crafted for television in subsequent decades.

The modes of capture and captivation deployed by television when it arrived did not rely on the affective logic of the spectral. Rather, television came to deploy different cultural technologies and techniques in soliciting the dispositions of its audiences. Central among these was the emergence of the notion of "the environment". This was so in the sense that the animal realities that natural history television aimed to capture were ones embedded in distinct nature milieus: milieus that were often presented as vulnerable and often in need of human protection if precarious animal lives were to be sustained. The spectral beasts of this chapter were no doubt objects of conservation in the sense that the cultural technologies and techniques with which they were captured were ones concerned with preservation. That is, with capturing marsupial bodies in order to preserve the animals' exhibitionary afterlife as trace, remnant or remainder. This, however, was a conservation that proceeded without "the environment" as rationale as it was to emerge in subsequent decades. And, as such, these spectral beasts could be framed by an ethos of preservation that could solicit sympathy for the suffering endured. Nevertheless, the animal and its milieu remained without a public. It was precisely this potential and emergent public that was to be triggered by "the environment" as it was subsequently figured in Australian natural history film, particularly as it was to emerge on public service television. We turn to this in the following chapter.

2
Captivating viewers
Early natural history television on the ABC

How did the natural history animal on the ABC emerge and how did it captivate audiences? These are the questions driving this chapter. In posing them, we reiterate our central argument that there was nothing natural about the natural history animal. It had to be crafted and assembled and, in this process, natural history animals were not only differentiated from other animals roaming the small screen but their capacity to affect viewers in distinct ways was also established. As we saw in the previous chapter, modes of capture shape the dynamics of captivation or the sense of being lured and bound to animals. The issue is: How did natural history animals lure audiences and how did they acquire the capacity to invite participation in emerging concerns about the environment and human–animal relations? In what ways did natural history animals on the ABC provoke new forms of civic interest and engagement?

One way to approach these questions would be to evaluate early animal content and representations on the ABC in terms of how well they expressed the ideals of public service broadcasting. This technique was rife in the organisation's annual reports. In early ABC *Annual Reports*, animal content on television was praised for informing children about the natural world or entertaining audiences with remarkable natural spectacles.[1] The assumption was that animals were simply one of myriad sources of content recruited in the service of the ABC Charter. However, this instrumental framing denies how ABC animals were constructed and how these creatures actually acquired the capacity to generate distinct forms of "public interest" or "national value".

In contrast to instrumentalism, we claim that some animal content on the ABC, particularly natural history programming, played a key role in shaping and constructing these values, in producing specific animal inflections for "public" and "national" interest. By captivating audiences in particular ways and inviting those audiences to gather around animals as interested or concerned publics, animals became devices of the public.[2] This term comes from recent debates in science and technology studies (STS) about how publicness and publics are enacted. For Marres and Lezaun, participation in publics is irreducibly material; it involves objects, devices or settings that have the capacity to engage or call into being diverse and idiosyncratic publics.[3] In relation to television, the sociotechnical capacity to visualise, frame and circulate content is quite literally an exercise in making things public. But it can also be an exercise in investing things with political or moral capacities or in identifying new problems that invite audiences to gather around a common concern and watch like a public. This important debate within STS highlights how publics are co-constituted with specific objects or concerns, how they are mediated, and how they involve various forms of association and political engagement.[4]

The natural history animal took a while to configure as a unique species capable of provoking new public interest and concerns. As the ABC began to make more locally-produced wildlife content from the mid-1960s on, animals were framed by various forms of authority as well as a range of problematisations about their habits and environments, and how humans were connected to them.[5] What we are particularly interested in in this chapter is the earliest framings

---

1 Australian Broadcasting Commission, *Annual Report*, 1959.
2 Marres and Lezaun 2011.
3 Marres and Lezaun 2011.
4 For investigations of the processes of public-making informed by STS, see Michael (2009). Also see Blue (2015) on multispecies publics and Hawkins (2013) on the ABC and public value.
5 Dibley and Hawkins 2019.

and expressions of animals as inhabiting "the environment": a hybrid place of complex natural and cultural interactions warranting care and protection. How were natural history animals implicated in shaping audiences' awareness of the environment? And how was this environmentalism linked to certain forms of nationalism?

Below we trace how animals became devices of the public on the ABC and the various forms of public interest and environmental awareness they generated. We begin with the challenges of making them visible, how the shift from radio to TV involved trials around remediation and the emergence of questions about *how* to make animals televisual. We then consider the screening of BBC wildlife content on the ABC in the 1950s and early 1960s. Through this period, most of the animal content on the ABC was imported from the BBC. This colonial legacy was formative in the development of ABC TV, but in the case of animal content it took a fascinating form. By looking closely at a 1956 episode of *Zoo Quest* (BBC, 1954–1964), one of David Attenborough's first TV series and screened on the ABC in 1960, it is possible to see how capturing animals in the wild on film was technically difficult. Early television camera techniques were no match for elusive modes of animal being. In deploying other devices to contain and display animals for TV, Attenborough provoked a form of viewing in which the sovereign human gaze ultimately prevailed. These public animals were entertaining, but they generally weren't problematic and they certainly didn't come from "the environment". We then examine *Dancing Orpheus* (ABC, 1962), one of the first animal documentaries made by the ABC in 1962. It used techniques of visual capture that displayed the lyrebird performing "in the wild" in what appeared to be a state of natural and spontaneous self-betrayal. However, in the final scenes this wild bird was problematised as vulnerable because it was living in an environment under threat. In this move, the bird shifted from an object of remarkable natural beauty performing for audiences to something demanding public care and concern.

The historical material we review shows animals as diverse devices of the public capable of provoking a variety of questions about what animals were, how they should be observed and why they mattered. It also shows that ABC animals were variously political and *a*political.

Not only did they become implicated in realising the governing logics of public service broadcasting through performances that generated new forms of popular entertainment and information, they also occasionally provoked encounters with audiences in which new relations between humans and animals were configured. Making animals public in the ABC triggered new human–animal contact zones in which both humans and animals were reconfigured in relation to one another. Sometimes this involved the activation of new forms of political attention in audiences who were invited to engage with animals and environments as a concerned public. And sometimes it involved complete *denial* about human–animal relations and realities, and the environments they inhabited. Animals were there to affirm human sovereignty, not question it, and so supported a mode of settler-national dwelling.

Televisual animals: Remediating radio beasts and importing BBC animals

Animals have a rich, enduring and largely unexamined history in Australia's national broadcaster. As radio developed, programs about animals emerged across a range of formats. In "Rural Broadcasts", various agricultural authorities discussed the role of industrial and working animals in the national economy; in "Talks and Discussions", experts explained the biology and behaviour of various species for explicitly pedagogic purposes; and in "Educational Broadcasts", animals were both instructive and amusing, offering a mix of "entertainment … [and] pleasant instruction" that often encouraged "children into their own gardens, paddocks and sea shore in search of everyday creatures".[6] Then there were the early forms of anthropomorphic animal celebrities such as "The Muddle-Headed Wombat" (ABC, 1951–1970), who featured on the ABC's popular radio serial *The Argonauts Club* and entertained children for decades. Subsequent shows that followed the "talks and discussion" format included the weekly series *News from Nature*, which, when it commenced in 1956, was directed by naturalist

---

6   Australian Broadcasting Commission, *Annual Report*, 1939, 37.

and journalist Alec Chisholm and included among its guest speakers ornithologists, botanists and entomologists from the country's key scientific organisations. The following year, the weekly series *Science Commentary* was also established with experts from CSIRO and the museum sector speaking to their specialism, including Ellis Troughten, Curator of Mammals at the Australian Museum. In 1958 the weekly series *Wild-life and the Countryman* was launched. This program featured Eric Worrell, the naturalist and herpetologist and founder of the Australian Reptile Park (est. 1948), who discussed topics as varied as the mutton-bird industry and how to contend with venomous snakes.

The sound ecologies of radio generated different mediations of animals and contrasting ways in which animals were both heard and spoken about. These radio ecologies generated diverse animals with an eclectic array of framings and experts accounting for them, from zoologists to amateur naturalists to farmers. Here animals were framed variously as economic resources by professionals in agriculture, as scientific objects located in the networks of zoologists and other experts, as contemplative objects for the ruminations of amateur naturalists, and as pedagogic objects and anthropomorphic subjects animating children's programming. The ABC's radio animals, through their mediation by various experts, were aligned with facts and enlivened with tales of discovery and adventure that were carried by the emotive swirl of music. These were informative animals revealing details of their biology, behaviour or economic worth to listeners. They were discursive animals, as the bearers of narrative, positioned in accounts of scientific discovery, of expeditionary adventure or economic modernisation. And they were sonic animals, as realities crafted from the soundscapes and spoken words through which they came to be performed. The absence of visual content meant that these animals were disembodied; they had to be represented by information and storytelling or by their calls and song. Making animals visible on television demanded a whole new set of authorisations and techniques that would establish the evidentiary force or credibility of animal performances and orient viewers to them in distinctive ways. These unique televisual techniques and framings took a while to emerge.

When television was first established at the ABC in 1956, it adhered to existing radio departments and programming classifications within the public broadcaster.[7] Format protocols for local productions were rolled over to the new medium, where the capacities of television quickly saw a refining but not necessarily a remaking of the cultural techniques established in radio. An early example of this process involved the remediation of the *Junior Farmer Competition*, a popular radio success. When this show was moved to television, various format changes ensued including the presence of live cattle, sheep and poultry in the TV studio, which competitors were asked to handle "before the television cameras".[8] This show, with its reliance on actual animals in the studio, was a remarkable experiment in visualising a radio format – it didn't last. While there is no explanation as to why the show was abandoned, it is not hard to speculate that the logistics of wrangling sheep and cattle in a TV studio may have been a key factor.

It was during the 1960s, as television increasingly ensconced itself in the domestic spaces, that wildlife began to proliferate across the nation's television screens. During this period local content was scarce on both public and commercial television, mostly due to the prohibitive costs of its production and distribution. The local content that was produced was largely broadcast live-to-air for technical and economic reasons. Television programming was imported, from the USA for the commercial channels and the UK for the public broadcaster. This trend held true for animal content. The commercial channels were dominated by American shows, exposing Australian audiences to the various formats in which animal content was presented on North American commercial television. For example, those screening on Channel 7 included the expeditionary documentary series *Kingdom of the Sea* (Emperor Production, 1957–1958), which focused on marine life and featured John D. Craig, adventurer, stuntman and diver, who revealed to audiences "the beauties and dangers of Earth's underwater worlds". Other broadcasts included the Canadian nature documentary series *Untamed World* (CTV, 1968–1976). In the mid-1960s, Channel 7 also broadcasted the popular series, Walt Disney's *True-Life Adventure*

---

7 Fitzsimons, Laughren and Williamson 2011, 59–60.
8 Australian Broadcasting Commission, *Annual Report*, 1959, 13.

feature films, whose spectacular anthropomorphic beasts were already familiar to Australian audiences with Hoyts Cinema having screened many of the films in the series nationally through the 1950s.[9] On Channel 9, broadcasts included the CBS series, *Zoorama* (San Diego Zoo, 1955), which explored how animals were captured for zoos in a show-and-tell format shot on location. Channel 10 screened *Animal World* (NBC). This wildlife documentary series was produced and hosted by Los Angeles-based Bill Burrud, and aired between 1968 and 1971. Episodes focused on particular animal behaviours and habitats with content from across the globe, including the episode, "Animal World: Life Downunder" (NBC, no date), where Channel 10's Sydney viewers got to watch Australian wildlife narrated by the Californian.

From the mid-1960s the commercial channels began to produce local animal content, which followed the action-orientated formats of American commercial television. Exemplary here was Channel 9's adventure documentary *The Shark Hunters* (Ron Taylor Productions, 1963). Filmed underwater at Tweed Heads, the Great Barrier Reef and southern New South Wales, this show mixed the safari/hunt format with the tradition of zoo collection films. Under the mantra, "bring 'em back alive", the film focused on the exploits of two shark hunters charged with collecting various shark specimens for aquariums. However, giving the animal adventure TV genre, exemplified by the *Lassie* series (CBS, 1954–1973), an Antipodean twist, it was with the children's series *Skippy the Bush Kangaroo* (Fauna Productions, 1968–1970) that Channel 9 made its most enduring and nationally and internationally successful investment in animal television.

In the first years of ABC TV, there was little locally-produced natural history content. When animals were on the small screen, they were usually BBC imports on whose programs the ABC had "first rights to take or decline".[10] In contrast to the televisual animals on commercial television, which had evolved more directly from early film and its narrative and visual conventions, BBC TV animals had lineages that connected them closely to their radio predecessors.[11]

---

9   See Disney nature film. *Weekly Times* 14 January 1953, 52. Disney's *The Olympic Elk* (1956) was broadcast by Channel 7 in November 1966.
10 Fitzsimons, Laughren and Williamson 2011, 60.

Exemplary here was one of the BBC's earliest television wildlife series *Look* (1955–1968), which the ABC broadcast in the early 1960s. *Look*'s chat-show format took its cues from popular BBC wildlife radio shows like Desmond Hawkins' *The Naturalist* (1946) and interspersed animal footage with interviews with wildlife cinematographers and amateur naturalists. However, over the 1960s many BBC wildlife programs rapidly moved out of the studio and into the field and provided popular content for the ABC. These early natural history programs often took their narrators on safari in search of exciting animal action that was considered more televisual. Foremost among the imported shows on the ABC was David Attenborough's first television series, *Zoo Quest* (BBC, 1954–1964), which followed the young naturalist's exploits in Guyana, Borneo and Paraguay collecting live animals for London Zoo.

Zoo Quest: Imperial interspecies intimacy

Zoo Quest is regarded as formative for the development of natural history television. Launching Attenborough's career, it also established many of the genre's conventions.[12] In developing the series, Attenborough's intention was to combine key elements of existing TV animal formats. These included the capriciousness of the live-to-air animal encounter, which had delighted audiences in a weekly television segment featuring a London zookeeper and his animals filmed in the BBC studio, and the "majestic and marvellous" qualities of wild animals "in their proper setting", which had been captured in popular animal safari shows shot on location.[13] In this way, *Zoo Quest* was both an evolution and break from an earlier genre of zoo films and from zoo TV shows.[14] Embedded in the tradition of the scientific expedition, *Zoo Quest* used the narrative device of the journey to structure each

---

11   See Bousé 2000; Chris 2006.
12   Bousé 2000; Chris 2006.
13   Attenborough 1980, 8.
14   For an account of the practices of filming in zoos and their relationship with the subsequent evolution of wildlife documentaries, see Horak (2006).

program. It was the adventure of finding and collecting the zoo-animal-to-be, rather than displaying the exhibited animal, that was the central focus. This shift meant that the narrative of each episode was driven by the promise of an animal encounter, of seeing animals in their natural states. For Attenborough, it was the thrill of an animal meeting in the wild that would captivate audiences and give the show "the spice of unpredictability".[15] This liveliness was emerging as central to the success of making animals televisual. While zoos provided captive examples of innumerable species close up, watching an animal sleeping in a cage or pacing up and down was not great television. TV was a visual and action-based medium; if animals were going to be interesting on the small screen, like earlier screen animals they had to be doing something.

In Episode 5 of the series, "Zoo Quest For a Dragon" (BBC, 1956), these dynamics can be seen at work. Attenborough and his entourage are in the jungles of Borneo searching for specimens to film and to collect – among them, orang-utans. The film crew and narrator wrestle with the contingencies of the jungle, the limits of their technology and varying degrees of co-operation from the apes.[16] In an early scene, Attenborough hacks his way through dense rainforest with a "native guide"[17] leading him to the elusive beasts. As he pushes through the undergrowth, he talks about orang-utans as exotic and elusive objects of curiosity and spectacle. "After an hour [of trekking]", Attenborough's hushed voice-over informs the audience, the first traces of the animal's presence are discovered. Discarded durian fruit and the primate's nest high up in the branches confirm the presence of the, as yet unseen, ape. This is then corroborated by the sound of "crashing in the branches ahead". Finally, and fleetingly, the arresting presence of the ape is glimpsed. Wide-eyed and staring up into the canopy, Attenborough and his guide "spot a great furry red form swaying in the trees". With this shot of the excited human observers, the film then cuts to the

---

15 Attenborough 1980, 8.
16 For the clip discussed here see: https://bit.ly/3sF6Ulz.
17 The authors have kept the term here to underscore that Attenborough continued in the habits of colonial expeditions.

orang-utan as it briefly and blurrily swings into shot, shrieking and largely obscured by thrashing branches.

The drama of this sequence is carried not by the visualisation of the orang-utan itself, which proved to be a very reluctant televisual subject, but by the voice-over and shots of Attenborough and guide gesturing excitedly. It is through this human enthusiasm that viewers are oriented to the eventual and very partial revelation of a swaying "great furry red form". What this sequence amplifies is that making orang-utans visual was technically difficult, if not impossible, to capture on film. In black-and-white footage viewers see brief, distant and out-of-focus images of the ape through violently shaking foliage. Nevertheless, the crafting of this televisual orang-utan through the suspense of its revelation overcomes these technical limitations. In seeking to activate viewers' curiosity, the sequence frames the animal as elusive, rarely seen and outside usual fields of human vision. The technique of the reveal in this early animal content relies not on holding the ape in the frame, on making it perfectly visible, but on tantalising viewers with the possibility of its appearance. In this sense, it is not that the ape is disappearing but that it is yet to appear – it is yet to be made fully visible and subordinate to the camera and, by proxy, the audience.

In a later scene from this episode, the orang-utan subject is crafted very differently. This scene offers a solution to the difficulties of making orang-utans visual. The camera in the jungle offered limited success in filming the wild ape, but subsequent scenes overcame this problem with the introduction of an additional, more familiar and decisive, device of capture – the cage. And, while the first scene gambled on the provocation of viewers' curiosity through the promise of the reveal, the second activates a pleasure in the ape's charismatic appeal that is contingent on the animal's own playful curiosity. Shot on board *Zoo Quest*'s expeditionary vessel, the cage scene focuses on Attenborough's interactions with an infant orang-utan that had been caught by locals and purchased as part of the expedition's collecting activities.[18] This orang-utan is not an elusive presence that the camera can barely capture but a completely compliant televisual subject. Unlike the sovereign

---

18   See Attenborough 1980, 211–12 for his account of the purchase and taming of the ape.

2 Captivating viewers

beast, the "man of the forest", that framed Attenborough's narration of the opening jungle sequence, this caged infant is thoroughly anthropomorphised and christened "Charlie". Under Attenborough's care, viewers witness Charlie's introduction into a regime of "dominance and affection".[19] However, Charlie is not simply a pet in the making, he is also a specimen. True to the trope of the colonial scientific expedition and associated collecting practices, the captive animal is brought into regimes of colonial knowledge and power as a zoological specimen. However, Charlie's scientific or wild value is not the dominant framing in this sequence; rather, it is his appeal as an affectionate and engaging televisual animal. Accompanied by a jaunty soundtrack, Attenborough's exchanges with the young ape embrace what Jamie Lorimer has described as a "playful aesthetic of interspecies intimacy".[20] This sequence capitalises on Charlie's simian charisma and orients viewers to him as a docile and fully visual and disciplined being available for human pleasure and affection. Even when he was framed as a zoological specimen, his public value was located more in his visual charisma than his value to science. When this episode was first aired on British television, keepers at the monkey house at London Zoo reported "a surge of visitors" in response to Charlie's appearance on *Zoo Quest*. Making Charlie visible meant turning him into an affective subject whose cuteness propelled him into animal celebrity.[21]

These two *Zoo Quest* sequences highlight the complexities of early attempts at making animals visual and public on the BBC. Both operate in affective registers, captivating the embodied viewer with the thrill of the reveal of an elusive wild primate seeking to escape encroaching humans, or entrancing the viewer with the charismatic appeal of the captured baby ape seeking out the comfort of human touch. In provoking certain modes of looking at and knowing animals and building audience interest in them, *Zoo Quest*'s orang-utans and their viewers were implicated in a double imperialism: one geopolitical in the sense that the right to collect specimens in colonial territories

---

19 Tuan 1984.
20 Lorimer 2015, 134.
21 On the practices of nonhuman charisma, see Lorimer (2007); on the "configurations of cuteness", see Genosko (2005).

went largely unquestioned; the other zoo-political, in the sense that human dominion over animals was assumed. In this way, *Zoo Quest* contributed to the enclosure of wildlife in the exhibitionary complex,[22] which, through a regime of "show and tell", adjudicated the boundary between the human and nonhuman animal. The effect of this was to activate a particular disposition in audiences that proceeded in the assurance of the human as sovereign and animals as performing *for* humans. However, this disposition was open to disruption by animal gesture.[23] As Charlie extended a hairy arm from behind the bars of his cage, the episode closed with a close-up of Attenborough's hand caressing the baby ape's. The pathos of the young orang-utan's reaching out to the human confirmed his subjectivity and established a scene of interspecies intimacy where the human–animal boundary and human superiority was, perhaps for a moment at least, disrupted.

When first screened on the ABC, *Zoo Quest* and other BBC imports were important in generating local audiences for wildlife content. However, while these BBC animals dominated the screen, they were animals poorly adapted to the ABC's national agenda and media milieu. Their performances did not translate the institution's mandate to show Australia to Australians. In this context, these imported animals could only point to a lacuna in the ABC TV's programming: where was the Australian animal? How was it being made visible and did it have a public?

The ABC animal and the emergence of environmental nationalism

Ironically, the BBC actually provided an early answer to these questions in Charles and Elsa Chauvel's travelogue, *Australian Walkabout* (BBC, 1959). When it was first broadcast on the ABC in 1960, this 13-part series brought the safari format to remote Australia, and Australian content to local screens. Filmed over 1957–1958 by the noted Australian filmmakers, and edited by the BBC for release in 1959, the series represented "the outback" through an Australian middle-class,

---

22 Bennett 1995.
23 Creed 2015.

urban optic for a British audience. It was then exported back to Australia where the ABC offered viewers visual access to remote Australia in a form mediated by a major British cultural institution. The narrative of the series walked an ambivalent line. Regularly marvelling at the modernisation of the landscape as it was industrialised for agriculture or mining, the show celebrated the indomitable settler spirit in "taming" wild and inhospitable space. However, it also lamented the inevitable loss of such places and their Indigenous inhabitants, both human and nonhuman, to processes of modernisation. While native animals were not central to the show, they did provide regular interest for the Chauvels and their viewers. Occasionally, these animals provoked expressions of concern for a disappearing or vulnerable nature that was not yet identified as "the environment". For example, in one episode Elsa Chauvel, surveying the fauna of the flood plains of northern Australia, lent her voice to an emerging call for conservation in which native flora and fauna and their habitat might be protected from the degradation caused by the commercial exploitation of natural resources: "Everywhere here animals and birds are prison free, how wonderful it would be if this country ... could be retained for them." This was a framing that stood in sharp contrast to the narratives of capture and confinement driving the BBC's safari-meets-zoo TV shows of the time. Rather, this notion of conservation sought to capture audiences with the romantic lure of an emancipated nature – one autonomous and free from any encroachment of the human.

In many ways, the sentiment behind the Chauvels' appeal to leave things alone so animals and birds could remain free resonated with an emerging environmental sensibility in Australia that was to gather momentum during the late 1960s and early 1970s. This was an implicitly political sentiment with two powerful dimensions. First, it engaged an environmental politics that sought to articulate "the political dimensions of concerns about the natural world and the place of people in nature".[24] Second, it engaged a nationalist politics integral to processes of decolonisation in former settler colonies in which a preference for native biota marked a distinct cultural break with empire.[25] In this context, "the environment" was becoming an emergent

---

24 Robin 1994, 3.

matter of concern and diverse publics were beginning to gather around it. The local ABC TV animal was enrolled in this project and became a device of the public, a creature that could provoke new interest in animals and new questions about their place in "the environment" rather than in the wild, the outback or in nature.

As we have mentioned, locally crafted ABC animals were rare in the 1950s. However, over the 1960s a number of specimens began to emerge in a variety of programs. Early examples included the ABC's first wildlife series, *Wildlife Australia* (ABC, 1962–1964), which was written by the ornithologist and radio broadcaster, Graham Pizzey, and produced with the CSIRO. Shows in this series took viewers into unique Australian environments, such as the Mallee country or Barmah forest, and provided a didactic explication of the native wildlife found in these habitats. However, as each show unfolded, what was revealed was not the spectacular animal body but the threats posed to these natural habitats by human encroachment. In the case of the episode, "Flooded Forest", viewers were informed of the devastating consequences of the commercial felling of red gums in Barmah, which, if unchecked, would "upset the balance of nature". It was through this format, which aimed to deliver a pedagogic account of a compelling nature always on the cusp of being spoiled by human activities, that a sense of civic duty was enlisted in viewers in the hope of ensuring their commitment to conservation policy. This approach was not only the preserve of ABC's early forays into nature documentary. Similar tactics marked other ABC TV formats that enrolled wildlife experts and conservationists to explicate native species and their precarious environments. The magazine show *Australia Today* (ABC, 1964), for example, included animal segments such as "Some Australian Birds with Harry Frith". Frith was a zoologist and director of the Wildlife Survey Section of the CSIRO, a popular writer on Australian natural history and expert advisor to state and federal governments on conservation policy. Other shows that offered variations on this emerging environmental nationalism included the science show *Around the Bush* (ABC, 1964), which starred naturalist and educator Vincent Serventy, out in the field, and *Wild Life Paradise: Australian*

---

25   Bennett 2017; Ginn 2008.

Fauna (ABC, 1967), which was filmed at the Sir Colin Mackenzie Sanctuary (later Healesville Sanctuary). As the recurring reference to Australia in these titles suggests, these early locally produced ABC animals were determinedly national. They were also predominately pedagogical, captivating audiences with their display of unique characteristics. More significantly, these creatures were nearly always animals that belonged to the environment, which was framed as a natural but imperilled network of relations warranting public attention and care to limit human intrusion and impacts.

Even so, the broader media ecology of the ABC was still dominated by imported animals. Local animal content as it emerged over the 1960s remained scarce and limited in reach. The national animal had yet to enrol its public. As nature filmmaker Ken Taylor contended, writing in the mid-1970s:

> For Australian viewers in the sixties wildlife, for the most part, happened somewhere else ... on safari in Africa or beneath the skeins of wild geese across the saltings and marshes of Europe. Throughout those years as we searched about for subjects to film for television, we had casually overlooked the natural history resources of a continent. Today this seems an extraordinary oversight, especially as we now make good natural history films with appeal for mass audiences in Australia and in other countries. Yet, through the sixties, the natural world was hardly considered as a relevant subject for Australian television. We failed to see beyond the tame kookaburras and kangaroos in the dusty "sanctuaries" of our last suburbs.[26]

However, as native fauna were increasingly enlisted in various ABC productions during the late 1960s and early 70s, they began to provoke growing interest in the continent's wildlife. This no doubt tapped into what Libby Robin charts as an emerging "ecological consciousness" that came to prominence in Australia over this period.[27] The question is: How did these ABC animals provoke new conceptions of and

---

26 Taylor 1976, 2.
27 Robin 1994.

concerns about the natural world? How did they displace established tropes of the colonial frontier, where animals were wild and menacing, and instead nurture ecological sensibilities in audiences that prioritised native animals as both valuable and vulnerable? This shift was significant. The natural environment, once represented as a passive resource for, or an impediment to, a modernising nation, was now problematised. This transition required new visual rhetorics that rejected the menace and the allure of "the outback" and colonial framings of nature and its fauna. Instead, articulations of environmental nationalism required a different landscape and different animals in order to captivate audiences and provoke new public interests and concerns.

Dancing Orpheus: Observing the animal body

One of the ABC's first wildlife documentary features, *Dancing Orpheus* (ABC, 1962), was pivotal in articulating this shift.[28] In moving now to a close analysis of this program, our focus is on how the lyrebird featured in it became a device of the public. How did its performance provoke new dispositions and modes of viewing; new modes of public engagement with animals and the environment? How did it come to lure and captivate its audience and imbue them with an environmental nationalist sensibility?

Celebrated for its visual and technical prowess in capturing the secretive superb lyrebird, *Dancing Orpheus* won an Australian Film Institute Gold Award in 1963 and a Diploma of Merit at the Melbourne Film Festival.[29] In framing lyrebirds as objects of ethological and aesthetic interest, the film invites the viewer to follow the camera as it seeks out the birds in Sherbrooke Forest, part of the Dandenong Ranges National Park on Melbourne's outskirts. The opening sequences involve awkward tracking shots of lyrebirds moving through the dense undergrowth of the forest. The viewer catches fleeting glimpses as the

---

28 It is unclear when this was first broadcast. According to the *TV Times*, it was screened twice in 1969; it may have aired earlier.
29 A clip from this film can be viewed at http://tinyurl.com/dadpc5ta.

2 Captivating viewers

camera tries to keep up with the birds as they run across the forest floor. There is no musical soundtrack. Instead, a sombre authoritative male narrator gives an account of the birds, their habits and habitat. The central narrative drive and tension comes from the account of the cock birds' elaborate courting display and mimicry; would the birds perform it for the camera, and more importantly, would the audience get to observe it? Like *Zoo Quest*, this framing worked to activate the audience's curiosity and orient them to the lyrebirds as interesting and, potentially, spectacular and beautiful. Then, in the penultimate sequence, the cock bird begins to dance. The camera is still as it films the display in mid shot. It is a remarkable visual performance of a vibrating bird body accompanied by the bird's very elaborate and resonant mating song. The narrator introduces the performance to the audience with the emphatic declaration: "*This* is the lyrebird: dancer, musician, mimic – a dancing Orpheus." In this verbal framing, the lyrebirds are anthropomorphised as accomplished artists, while the vision captures them as embodiments of pure natural expression.

The effect was to situate the birds "in the wild" as if the realism of their performance was simply out there awaiting capture; the opening sequences of the camera searching for the birds amplified this. Throughout the film, the lyrebirds are encountered seemingly unmediated by humans in the sense that traces of the latter are excised from the vision. Pristine in undisturbed nature, the lyrebirds are presented as if discovered by the camera and revealed to the audience for the first time. However, full, unhindered vision is not readily on offer; the birds are elusive, constantly obscured. Jumpy tracking shots and the absence of music enhance the effect of the birds evading visual capture and the difficulties of the camera finding and keeping up with them. It also recalls the chase scenes endured by earlier screen animals. These are birds that do not want to be seen. Meanwhile, the viewer is waiting and watching in anticipation of satisfying vision of the bird's body.

In the courtship dance sequence a quite different camera technique is used. Concealed within a hide, a fixed camera films as the bird comes into the field of vision. The camera is still: passive in the face of the animal body, which was perfectly visible in a clearing *performing itself.* The effect is of a remarkable natural event serendipitously observed. For the audience, this technique evokes the generative thrill of the hidden camera, a sense of seeing without being seen, of an intimacy without reciprocity. This thrill also amplifies a stark distinction between the observer and the observed, between subject and object. The struggle for visual mastery now accomplished, the bird's body is revealed in its full performance.

The materiality of the lyrebird's body is central to the pleasure of this sequence. As Anat Pick notes,[30] fascination with the animal body has been a key trope in the history of cinema and, of course, in the emergence of wildlife television. But in *Dancing Orpheus* this pleasure is not just related to the incitement of curiosity about this body and the audience's desire to see it. It also comes from the way in which the ontology of the bird, its unique manners of being, establishes an affinity with the ontology of the camera: its capacity to register and react to the materiality of the bird's body and transmit it to a public. This affinity or mutual attunement of the bird and the medium enacts a lyrebird reality *and* documentary realism in the same moment. Enactment is a stronger term than shaping or constructing. It points to a significant scepticism about essential realities and an insistence on the ways in which ontologies, both animal and technical, have to be done in situ and in relation. The perfect mid shot of the courtship dance, of the bird in the centre of the frame vibrating in complete visibility, its song resonating, provokes a sense of direct witnessing of the liveliness of animal being unfolding in real time and space. The camera isn't just looking at things – it is looking at *things happening* and this enhances its technical authority as a device of accurate visual observation. Of course, in the messy world of TV production and filmmaking, hours and hours of footage of nothing much would have been shot in order to get this sequence, that was then assembled with editing, narration and much more. However, in the natural history genre that was emerging in the ABC at the time, the lyrebird could not be just a bird; it had to be a bird performing its unique natural being in full visibility of the camera, a bird becoming televisual and public.

There is no question that in making the lyrebird televisual its performance was elaborately crafted and purified. This was an

---

30   Pick 2007.

enactment of an animal reality that worked hard to excise the messy network of relations in which the lyrebirds were embroiled in order to frame them as pure, natural entities. The specific birds filmed in *Dancing Orpheus* were well-known and had long been the focus of ornithologists whose expertise during the production process was critical. Not only had these particular lyrebirds been the subjects of intensive field observations for at least two decades, the cock bird featured in *Dancing Orpheus* was also familiar to many Melbournians. At the time of filming he was a longstanding celebrity of Sherbrooke Forest, and was distinguished by a rather more vernacular name, "Spotty".[31] Over his 22 years he had become an attraction at Sherbrooke Forest and a key reason to visit the nature reserve. *Dancing Orpheus* withheld the fact that Sherbrooke Forest was a nature reserve on the edge of Melbourne's suburban sprawl and a popular destination for the city's daytrippers, and no mention was made of Spotty's popularity. Instead, the film isolated the bird from these imbroglios in order to make him a televisual animal performing its pure and natural essence. Poignantly, the bird's television debut proved to be a swan song of sorts. Spotty disappeared shortly after *Dancing Orpheus* was produced.[32]

How was this televisual animal authorised and accounted for? What techniques and forms of reasoning were used to make this performance plausible, to make audiences accept that this was the natural truth of lyrebirds? Accountability processes constitute worlds and ways of knowing them. In the case of *Dancing Orpheus* there is no question that the film captures the generative force of animal being. The cock's dance is framed as a remarkable natural expression, as inherently aesthetic, and this aesthetic is inseparable from the material possibilities embodied in the animal. Beyond the expressive capacities of the bird, this framing is also successful because it activates the aesthetic disposition of the viewer who recognises the bird as naturally beautiful and, in doing so, accepts this aesthetic mode of being as an accountable lyrebird reality.

Accounting for the lyrebird dance as pure natural expression was a very particular way of making it public. In this very early example

---

31 Robin 2007, 131–2.
32 Robin 2007, 132.

of Australian wildlife documentary there is not a lot of science to authorise this animal reality. Lyrebirds are not fully anchored in scientific positivism. The mating display and other habits are explained as distinctive behavioural traits unique to this species, but the dominant framings are about the extraordinary aesthetics of natural performance and the power of television to capture it. *Dancing Orpheus* enacts and affirms not just an aesthetic reality for lyrebirds but also an emerging capability in television to make visible new and exciting Australian animal realities. However, towards the end of the film another mode of accounting for the bird briefly emerges. The film closes with a warning about the bird's legal status as a protected species. This is a fleeting but powerful acknowledgement of the imbroglios that compromise the natural purity of lyrebirds. In raising this issue, the lyrebird on screen becomes a matter of concern; its body is beautiful *and* vulnerable. This implicitly conservationist framing provokes another disposition in viewers: a sense of obligation to nonhuman others with whom they are inextricably entangled. Having established the lyrebird as an aesthetic object captured for human pleasure and edification, in the final moments this distanced subject–object or human–animal relation is disrupted by making the audience aware of their responsibility to care and conserve. With this gesture the lyrebird is enrolled in a national environmental agenda. In contrast to *Zoo Quest*'s orang-utans, who are enlisted in the last gasps of an imperial nature, the lyrebirds of *Dancing Orpheus* are framed as part of a newly national nature and its emerging environmentalist agenda. These birds are devices of the public; they call into being new publics and invite new forms of collective engagement and concern with animals and environments.

Conclusion: The "properly observed" animal

In 1970 the ABC Features Department produced the watershed series *Bush Quest with Robin Hill*.[33] It starred the artist and naturalist Robin Hill as he observed and sketched the wildlife of central and coastal Victoria. This series was pivotal to the institutional history and

---

33   Inglis 1983, 289.

emergence of the ABC animal. It charted the artist/naturalist's exploits by rowboat, pushbike and horseback in regional Victoria, where traditionally iconic marsupials – "roos and koalas" – were shunned in favour of wetland birds and marine mammals, which were cast as precarious entities located in vulnerable environments. According to Ken Taylor, *Bush Quest*'s director, the series established a new audience for Australian wildlife, breaking with earlier presentations of the bush and cultivating a new environmental ethos sensitive to nature's vulnerability, to its fragility.[34] The series was also markedly different from the travelogues and expeditionary films that mediated an earlier colonial nature. It made rarely witnessed national animals visible and public and located them in "the environment", which was now becoming an object of national and political concern.

The series' critical and public success was also instrumental in the establishment of the ABC Natural History Unit in the early 1970s. The first program in the unit's long-running series of programs badged "Wild Australia" built on the *Bush Quest* formula. It used the dual perspectives of the aesthetic and the scientific to mediate animals and their environments. This time, however, these perspectives were not embodied in the single figure of the artist/naturalist but in an ongoing screen dialogue between an artist and a scientist. The zoologist, Douglas Dorward, and artist, John Olsen, fronted the first series of "Wild Australia" (1972). Their respective expertise and sensibilities mediated nonhuman animal worlds for ABC viewers, which were also enhanced by technical advances in TV production.[35] On his involvement, Olsen reflected:

> The interesting thing about the film is that it shows people how new and unusual our environment is – how little we know about it. For example, you go up to Arnhem Land where a lot of mining companies are drilling and wrecking the landscape – and the scientists are still uncertain of the creatures, the birds, the insects,

---

34 Taylor 1976.
35 Aesthetically and technically accomplished, *Wild Australia* was also significant as an early colour ABC production anticipating the 1975 arrival of colour television.

the animals that are in the area ... The sum total of it is that we still don't know our own environment .... We still have a lot of work to do to know our own place and be part of it. ... [Judith Wright] puts it: "All we want out of the countryside is dollars. We are still a frontier civilisation, still mowing the place down to make money from it. I'll begin to believe we are indigenous when we begin to act out of love for it." So what happens with this film, what makes it so extraordinary, is that we are seeing things that have not been properly observed before.[36]

What is significant here is the claim for "the properly observed" animal and environment, which is an optic that is as much cultural as it is technical and scientific. It is a way of narrating and seeing the nonhuman world through an environmental nationalism, which was to come to situate not only native animals but settler subjects in their "proper" place. In this context, ABC animals were significant as devices of the public. Via certain techniques of visualisation, performances and framings, they came to evoke particular issues and concerns that cohered around articulations of environmental nationalism. In doing so, they assembled a distinct public, one which, as Olsen put it, was prepared to do the work of knowing "our own place and be[ing] part of it". In the following section we explore in detail how such televisual animal realities were crafted; in particular, we examine the ways in which such performances of wildlife came to be provoked.

---

36   Cited in Laurie Thomas (1972). Spotlight on the untouched Australia. *Australian*, 16 May. Australian Broadcasting Corporation Archives, Melbourne, 11/5779.

Part Two: Provoking

How does the material reality of animals become a televisual reality? In Part Two we consider a range of examples from the earliest days of the ABC's Natural History Unit (NHU) to the 2000s, which explore how a natural history animal is produced and crafted. Our aim, however, is not to go backstage and expose how contrived or artificial natural history animals on television are, to show that they aren't really that natural after all. This is taken as a given. Instead, our focus is on the various ways in which natural history animals are made convincing and believable on television, how the effects of "reality and truth, authority and plausibility" are realised in this very particular context.[1] In Jean-Baptiste Gouyon's account of the emergence of the BBC Natural History Unit, he argues that putting animals on the small screen not only built public interest and curiosity in animals, it also helped establish the authority of television as a source of trusted factual information.[2] Television enabled audiences to gain privileged access to the natural world and to learn more about it; to connect seeing and viewing to understanding. However, in order for this institutional authority to be established, nature and animals had to become objects of knowledge, they had to

1 Frow 2006, 2.
2 Gouyon 2011, 431.

acquire "evidential value".³ The question is how? How were animals to be represented and known? What kinds of evidence would elicit convincing natural history performances and how could this information be entertaining not just educational?

The examples we explore in the following two chapters offer various answers to these questions. They show how the processes of visualising and representing animals over the evolution of the ABC's NHU, and in wildlife TV more widely, generated shifting performances and authorisations. In Chapter 3 we begin with some examples from the early 1970s when locally-made natural history programs on the ABC were emerging as a new and appealing genre and the idea of what would count as a natural history animal was under development. We then consider a program made by the NHU in 1982 when it was an established and highly respected production unit and various genre conventions were more settled. Key documents investigated include the 1973 shooting diary of the Australian natural history cameraman, David Parer AO, when he was in the field filming the four-part series *Wildlife of Papua New Guinea* (ABC, 1975), and reflections from scientists and artists who were recruited by the ABC to enhance natural history productions. These reflections explore the epistemological and pedagogic objectives of various programs and the challenges of getting actual animals to realise these. This empirical material offers rich insights into the complexities of composing a natural history animal and genre: the vast material and institutional networks involved and the kinds of logistical, aesthetic and epistemic issues that emerged in making these animals televisual and public.

In Chapter 4 we explore "The Making of David Attenborough's Conquest of the Skies" (Colossus Productions, 2014), which was produced by Sky TV, one of Europe's leading media and entertainment companies, and shown on the ABC in 2015. This program was screened as the final episode in the high quality or blue chip natural history series *David Attenborough's Conquest of the Skies* (Atlantic Productions, 2014), a series about the evolution of flight. Episode 4 was promoted as offering rare "behind the scenes" insights into how the series was created. Making-of documentaries (MODs) have been on the increase

---

3   Gouyon 2019, 2.

over the last 25 years. They are symptomatic of what Jan Teurlings describes as the rise of "the society of the machinery", or a major mutation in popular culture in which the self-evidence of representations is debunked and audiences are invited to look beyond appearances and engage with the technical and organisational aspects of media production.[4] "The Making of David Attenborough's Conquest of the Skies" documents the technological sophistication and complexities of wildlife production in the 21st century and the unpredictable agency of the animal body. It shows how domesticated whooper swans were used to explain the aerodynamics of flight: to perform a scientific fact over and over again until they got it televisually right. Central to this program is the transformation of domesticated working animals into objectified natural history animals, fully disciplined by the demands of the genre. In the official episode, the natural history animal appears on screen occupying a self-contained natural world made available thanks to the wonders of television. In the MOD, the conditions of production surrounding this televisual animal are revealed and celebrated as a significant technical and collective achievement. There is a fascinating interplay between the process of provoking animals to perform, as shown in the MOD, and their ultimate performance in a nature that isn't found but carefully crafted and realised.

In exploring these cases, the primary concept driving our analysis is *provoking* or intervening to trigger an effect. Provocation challenges the idea that natural history television observes and represents an unconfined reality. As we saw in the previous chapter with the case of *Dancing Orpheus* (ABC, 1962), the idea of television offering direct observation of animals was an early and potent cultural effect that prefigured the rise of the ABC's NHU. The connections between the effect of direct observation and objectivity are powerful; however, in *Dancing Orpheus* these connections were highly orchestrated. The audience experience and visual effect of virtual witnessing of the lyrebird being its remarkable natural self was exactly that: a reality effect not an animal essence. Provocation foregrounds how these representations and effects are achieved, how the activity of television

---

4   Teurlings 2013, 518.

production has to be understood as an incitement, an event that calls forth and enacts various animal realities. These realities are always partial and are crafted according to various institutional expectations and cultural codes. The critical point is that the idea of *provoking* reality highlights how natural history animals are enacted and staged rather than found and documented. Making animals public on television was an exercise in extensive and multiple relays of technical intervention, creativity and mediation. These relays provoked very particular animals that became central to shaping the natural history genre. They also provoked animals that acquired distinct cultural and social force as they circulated in public networks, interacted with audiences and encouraged them to be affected by their distinct modes of being.

3
Developing the natural history genre
How animals and the media apparatus interact

How were natural history animals provoked on the ABC during the 1970s and 80s? What cultural conventions and reality effects shaped these provocations? One way to approach these questions is to turn to wider debates about genre. Invoking genre does not mean that we see "natural history" simply as a set of formulaic conventions for representing animals. Genres are far more complex and powerful than this. As John Frow notes, the most critical aspect of genre is the way in which it shapes representational practices and forms of knowledge.[1] The challenge is to understand exactly what those practices and knowledges are, how they are generated and their effects. Descriptors like "natural history" or "wildlife TV" are classifying statements, and a key function of genre is to categorise and establish boundaries. Genre classifications are not passive; they have to be enacted or done. For Frow, the potency of a genre emerges in the relations between texts and readers:

> Genre is neither a property of (and located "in") texts, nor a projection of (and located "in") readers: it exists as a part of the relationship between texts and readers, and it has a systemic existence. *It is a shared convention with a social force.*[2]

---
1   Frow 2006, 2.
2   Frow 2006, 102 (our emphasis).

Genres, then, are grounded in social institutions and shared conventions and codes; they guide expectations about what is considered plausible and appropriate for specific cultural forms. They also highlight how a classification like "natural history TV" was not self-evident but had to be created and realised through myriad practices and networks that stabilised this classification over time and gave it credibility.

However, while genre is a useful starting point for our analysis of how the natural history animal was provoked and codified, it does have some problematic limits. The danger with investigating natural history animals and television purely in genre terms (or as a televisual "format") is that it can implicitly privilege an anthropocentric analysis in which animals are reduced to textual effects. They become the passive expressions of cultural codes and classifications rather than active participants in materialising and shaping genre dynamics. Anat Pick argues that genre obscures the specificity of unique cinematic inscriptions and the ways in which filmmaking is an engagement with the world.[3] While this critique is powerful in its attention to material and animal worlds and their force in filmmaking, it does not hold up so well with television, which is driven by highly structured programming conventions and the economic imperative to classify.

Genre and formats matter in the production and economic contexts of television. However, this doesn't mean that they are all determining, as Pick assumes. Television production practices still have to engage with the world and with animal modes of being. So, when it comes to tracing the development of the natural history animal and genre, the challenge is to be attentive to the ways in which animals not only convey meaning but actively shape it.[4] Animals may have been provoked in much natural history television production, incited to perform natural facts or specific behaviours according to specific cultural codes, but they were also provocateurs. Their material and expressive capacities were often powerful determinants of what was filmed and how. In order to transcend the limitations of genre theory and its anthropocentric and textual bias, we are interested in how the

---

3   Pick 2007.
4   Smaill 2014.

3 Developing the natural history genre

natural history genre was materialised, how the habits and bodies of animals were encountered and negotiated in the process of making television and how these encounters shaped what would count as a credible and entertaining natural history animal.[5]

However, as much as we may want to stick to the animals, comprehensive information about their presence and role in NHU production processes in the 1970s and 80s is scarce. In our archival research, detailed descriptions about encounters with animals surfaced as very occasional and almost accidental asides. Animals appear almost as minor elements in a vast apparatus of film crews, funding negotiations, post-production practices, ratings data, program reviews and much more. This vast network of participants and interactions, that is "TV production" in action, confirms analyses within science and technology studies (STS) about how visual representations are produced and how meaning is made and circulates. As Luc Pauwels notes:

> Every representational process involves a translation and conversion of some kind; a process of inscription, transcription and/or fabrication whereby the original source (phenomenon, concept) is captured, transformed, or even (re-) created through a chain of decisions that involves several actors ... technological devices, and normative settings. This complex process of meaning-making has an important impact on what can be known and how, on what is revealed or obscured and on what is included or excluded.[6]

Our encounter with the archives documented this complexity and revealed constant internal debate and technical experimentation within the NHU about how to find and visualise animals, which aspects of them should be displayed and how the authority and evidential

---

5   See Belinda Smaill's (2014) exploration of the performance of animals in recent documentary films and her argument that the magnetism and active force of the animal body often exceeds the anthropocentricism of representational strategies.
6   Pauwels 2005, 4.

significance of these performances could be established. This archival material also exposed the huge diversity of visualising and epistemological practices involved (from editing to scientific advice to laying down a soundtrack) and how categories like "observing" or "representing" don't get anywhere near capturing these myriad sociotechnical and cultural practices.[7]

How, then, were animals corralled into the category "natural history" and what happened to them when they got there? And how did the natural history genre and animal become so authoritative and powerful in the ABC? By powerful we mean possessing significant cultural credibility as expressions of authentic animal modes of being. What patterns of meaning framed natural history animals and how did these meanings become durable and dominant? How did they establish what a natural history animal was in relation to public broadcasting? And what kinds of ontological politics did these animals provoke – how did they constitute very distinct species boundaries between humans as observers and animals as observed? We pursue these questions by looking at three practices that were central to provoking the natural history animal in the ABC over the 1970s and 80s and to shaping genre conventions: mediating, accounting and entertaining. Central to our analysis is the ways in which animals were implicated in these practices and configured them in certain ways.

Mediating animals: Filming a natural history animal

According to Gouyon, the origins of the natural history genre are deeply connected to the rise of ethology and the amateur naturalist.[8] Early natural history shows on the BBC front staged the naturalist out in the field patiently waiting and observing "wild" behaviour without intervention. Animals behaving unaware of cameras amplified the effect of indexicality and observational realism.[9] This commitment to human nonintervention was central to convincing audiences that

---

7 Lynch 2005, 27.
8 Gouyon 2019.
9 Gouyon 2019, 7.

3 Developing the natural history genre

animal behaviours were essential, natural and real. It also reinforced the idea of the camera as facilitating direct access to the world. It wasn't a mediating device; it was a technology of witness and documentation. During the 1960s the amateur naturalist as narrator and authority on the animal behaviour on display was gradually displaced by other experts, and visualisation practices became more sophisticated. However, direct observation of animal behaviour remained a dominant visual technique and cultural code of the developing genre.

Gouyon's historical account is compelling and empirically rich. The development of natural history programs on the ABC follows many of the patterns he outlines. However, one element of his argument that requires interrogation is the idea of noninterference with nature. In Gouyon's analysis, the camera is represented as a device for "mechanical objectivity".[10] While he acknowledges this representation as an effect of early natural history visualisation practices, as a key factor in authorising animal realities on TV as authentic, he does not interrogate it. The camera remains largely unexamined as a critical actant in the production of images. The natural history camera operator is acknowledged as needing the skills of an amateur naturalist: patience, field craft and dedication;[11] however, the vast assortment of technologies and devices central to enabling him to be in "the field" and central to seeking out and visualising animals is not explored. Yet these technologies and practices mediate; they "transform, translate, distort and modify the meaning or elements they are supposed to carry".[12] What the idea of noninterference obscures is the "ontological priority of mediation";[13] the way in which to look and record is to actively reach into the world and provoke it in certain ways.

The issue of "noninterference" in animals brings us to the shooting diary of the pioneering ABC wildlife cameraman and producer, David Parer AO.[14] This diary was written in 1973 when Parer was filming

---

10 Gouyon 2019, 7.
11 Gouyon 2019, 102.
12 Latour 2005a, 39.
13 Bowker 2010.
14 This is one of David Parer's earliest shoots for the NHU. He took up filming while doing scientific research and studying in Antarctica in 1970 and 1972; on his return, he joined the newly formed Natural History Unit. He went on

Episode 1 of a four-program series titled *Wildlife of Papua New Guinea* (ABC, 1975). These programs eventually went to air in March 1975, as part of the newly badged NHU series "Wild Australia". Under the "Wild Australia" brand, diverse content was made throughout the 1970s, not all of it focused on Australia. Programs based in places where Australia had close colonial or scientific ties, such as Papua New Guinea and Antarctica, were also screened.

Between October and December 1973 Parer travelled to the south-west corner of Papua New Guinea in order to get footage of the rusa deer (*Cervus timorensis*), an introduced species roaming the vast plains surrounding the Bensach River. Episode 1, "The Immigrant Deer", explored the deer and their habitat. The post-production film script described the show like this: "The film looks at the interacting wildlife – the aggregations of waterbirds, the marsupials, birds of prey, goannas and in particular the rusa deer which were introduced from Java in the 1920s, have thrived, and now number many thousands."[15] Parer's shooting diary is titled "Field Notes", implicitly referencing both anthropological and naturalist research practices. This document is a rare find in the NHU Archive. It offers a detailed description of the logistics of finding and filming animals in the wild. What gives it particular force are the insights it provides into the practical difficulties of filming in very remote places. Trying to negotiate unpredictable wild animals and a constantly changing environment produces endless frustration from waiting for "animals to perform", as Parer describes it. Parer's field notes are preoccupied with the weather, the tedium of hoping that animals will show up and do something interesting, the meals his local assistants prepared, and the myriad other technical, human and environmental challenges of the shoot.

These field notes are also an account of mediation in action. They describe some of the key processes involved in translating animals in

---

to become a highly awarded natural history cinematographer, shooting many of the NHU's programs including *Nature of Australia*. See his personal website https://davidparer.com/films_awards/ for a full list of his programs and awards.

15 "Post Production Film Script – Wildlife of Papua New Guinea, The Immigrant Deer". Produced by David Parer. ABC NHU Archive, Box 11/1427.

the wild into televisual animals. One of the challenges in analysing them is establishing what is meant by mediation. In media studies, mediation often refers to the ways in which a medium develops specific techniques of communication according to its technical and cultural organisation. But close readings of this diary make it impossible to reduce mediation to the effects of discrete media, to a process simply dominated by the demands of television. Televisual technologies and existing cultural conventions about filming animals are important, but to privilege these ignores the many layers and practices of mediation involved in this shoot. What Parer's field notes reveal are the complex and multiple interactions between technical agency, animal agency and human agency. Mediation emerges as a hybrid process involving diverse elements that mutually influence one another. Consider Parer's account of filming on Wednesday, 17 October 1973:

> Up at 5 am to medium rain and went into the hide. Got some very good stuff of spoonbills feeding, but sadly found that the 85 filter from the 300mm lens had fallen out along the way ... I am spending the day in the plain hide hoping the deer will come in to drink during the afternoon ... Well this afternoon has been the first real success of the trip. The deer came in in their hundreds along each side of the water, to within 20 yards of the hide ... It was later afternoon by the time they approached – I am told this is normal – and I shot mainly feeding shots with some fighting and grass in the antlers material. Some good portraiture material. Will attempt again for behavioural footage tomorrow. Out of the hide at 6.30 pm and took the sunset with waterbirds flying across its disk – plains area atmosphere.[16]

Parer is describing the micro-dynamics of mediation; he is giving an account of intimate interactions between multiple elements. He may place himself at the centre of the narrative, but his human actions are defined and extended through the camera he is using with its technical problems and complexities. Then there is the hide constructed to give him good visual access without being seen and the animals that finally

---

16 Parer, "Field Notes". ABC NHU Archive, Box 11/1427, no page numbers.

emerge and engage in "behaviours" or offer "good portraiture material". The sunset and "plains area atmosphere" are also central, signalling an aesthetically powerful visual effect. It is difficult to identify a passive reality awaiting capture and representation in this excerpt because there are multiple realities all affecting one another. It is also difficult to argue that this is a description of a reality being constructed as if each element is simply a means to an end and remains unchanged in the process. A reality is emerging, but it is an effect of provocations, of various devices and practices interacting and intervening in the world. Parer's field notes capture the inventive dimensions of mediation, the ways in which the televisual animal is not prior to mediation but an outcome or effect of it. He is confirming what Geoffrey Bowker describes as the inseparability of mediation and reality.[17]

But where is "natural history" in all this? This classification and institutional framing obviously justified and funded the shoot, but how is it being done in this excerpt? How is a genre being realised? Natural history is not mentioned in Parer's description, but it is possible to get a sense of its semiotic force in the way that he sees the animals and decides what and when to film. Parer is not interested in the spoonbills, he is interested in them *feeding*. He is also thrilled with the arrival of deer "in their hundreds" coming close to the hide, fighting and providing the opportunity for both dramatic and intimate portrait shots. The deer are massed in a visually spectacular way, and they are active and interactive. All these descriptions implicitly invoke the cultural conventions of natural history television: the styles and codes that had become privileged in making a televisual animal reality and truth. This genre is embedded in an ontological domain where animals are usually busily engaged in their natural behaviours, performing as representatives of their species; where they are often spectacularly grouped for great visual drama and also marked by unique or individual character traits that can be captured in close-up. This is the sort of animal that is constantly referenced in natural history and that gives the genre plausibility.

Parer brings to this encounter a mode of seeing that frames these animals in natural history ways. The animals may well have done many

---

17   Bowker 2010.

3 Developing the natural history genre

other things beyond feed and fight, they may have also done nothing much, but what Parer and the camera notice are the actions that confirm the framing. Parer's point of view is oriented to the cultural expectations and demands of the genre. Genre is provoking and realising this reality at the same time as genre confirms the presence of a pre-constituted world that supports it. This is a world where wildlife are expected to perform their essential species being, where they are defined by interesting "natural" behaviour that is observable. Frow describes the reality effects of genre like this: "The semiotic frames within which genres are embedded implicate and specify layered ontological domains – implicit realities which genres form as a pre-given reference, together with the effects of authority and plausibility which are specific to the genre."[18] When these deer perform natural behaviours, the objective reality of "nature" is simultaneously referenced and realised.

The camera is central to Parer's account. Throughout his field notes there are constant descriptions of its presence and demands: its heaviness, its noise which occasionally startles the animals, its vulnerability to sudden showers that can lead to hours of careful drying out, its mechanical faults. The camera isn't an instrument that Parer wields, it is an actant that both shapes and extends his agency and attaches him to the animals. The camera is a critical mediator that enables a relational unfolding between Parer and the animals. It is not simply connecting them but provoking a very distinct form of intra-action[19] in which humans and animals are mutually constituted as different and distinct: subject and object, observer and observed. In this sense, mediation doesn't presuppose or come between pre-existing subjects and objects, it actively configures these categories and establishes how they will interact.

At the same time, Parer also activates and realises the capacities of the camera as an observational device with distinct ontological effects. These capacities are not neutral or fixed technological functions; they are not about medium specificity, they are sociotechnical and culturalised.[20] That is, they are co-opted and adapted to realise

---

18 Frow 2006, 19.
19 Barad 2007.

particular cultural demands and figurations. Of course, the camera prescribes certain usages and constrains actions, but the way Parer deploys the camera is central to enacting its authority as a device that supposedly documents an objective reality. Consider this entry from his field notes for Tuesday, 23 October 1973:

> Spoonbills at the waterhole again but didn't come close in to the hide ... tried out the camera on the floor of the 6 ft elevated hide with the 300 mm lens on. Wind as usual gusty to about 20 knots. Too much camera movement. So we set to more bracing of the structure. Was into the completed hide about 1pm for the rest of the day. Deer stayed off the end of the long grass during the afternoon, a little reticent to come into the hide area. They came in about 5.30 but fairly heavy overcast – the 10 ft elevation gives a good perspective to be intercut with the low angle stuff given by the other hide.[21]

The hide is also playing a significant role here. These purpose-built structures are central to much scientific and amateur animal observation and to wildlife filming; they function to reduce human presence in what is under observation. Hides are assumed to facilitate human detachment and distance in order to ensure that animal behaviour will be unaffected by observation, that it will be "normal" and ordinary. Parer's filmmaking practices in the Bensach River are totally dependent on hides: these don't just disguise his body, they enhance the cultural techniques and authority of the camera as a device that captures reality happening before it. But the camera is being operated; Parer is attentive to angles and light and vibration, and he is already planning editing styles in which different elevations will be intercut in order to render the footage aesthetic and interesting to audiences. It's difficult to claim that these animals are simply *being witnessed*; they are emerging and being crafted as natural history objects through very particular sociotechnical and cultural practices. Setting up and preparing observational fields, deploying cameras in

---

20 Winthrop-Young 2013.
21 Parer, "Field Notes". ABC NHU Archive, Box 11/1427, no page numbers.

3 Developing the natural history genre

particular ways, disguising human and technical presence, establishing multiple points of view, all these techniques are amplifying the ontology of the camera as providing direct empirical access to an objective animal reality. They are also establishing the protocols and evidential significance of what is visualised: how these animals will be accounted for as real, as completely separate from humans and going about their natural ways.

These excerpts from Parer's field notes resonate with STS accounts of experimentation and the process of crafting of realities in laboratory settings.[22] The Bensach River could be considered as a vast outdoor laboratory or fieldwork site in which Parer, his local assistants and numerous other elements – from the camera to the weather – are engaged in practices of provoking animals. Some of these practices were deliberately interventionist – for example, the use of carcasses to attract animals is regularly described – while others were more subtle, but they were all designed to provoke a natural history animal reality. The field notes give rare insights into the messy day-to-day activities of shooting animals in the wild and highlight how a televisual animal begins to emerge.

Other documents show how these animals were subsequently shaped and transformed over time. In a long report sent back with the film cannisters to the producers and editors back in Melbourne, Parer outlines the behavioural aspects of the deer he observed for weeks.[23] These notes could easily pass as scientific descriptions with their extensive detail on the size of the reproductive herds, mating behaviours and daily patterns of movement across the plains. There is also rich ethnographic description outlining how the locals relate to the deer. This information is designed to orient the post-production staff to the footage in very particular ways and to indicate possible visual languages for the edits and narrative framings. Parer's suggestions move

---

22 Latour and Woolgar 1986.
23 This report has no title, just the heading: "Rather undisciplined rambling notes and ideas". Parer sent the report back to the ABC NHU office along with film cannisters of unedited footage. On the front of the document was a letter explaining that it also included shot lists and suggestions for edits. Located in ABC NHU Archive, Box 11/1427.

between the scientific, the aesthetic, the ethnographic and the intertextual. Consider his suggestion on how to edit the opening panorama introducing the vast plains and grazing deer to the audience: "would love to capture that feeling of openness and freedom of the opening pan in 'Wake in Fright', taken in Central Australia; that's the idea anyway".[24]

In the post-production script for "The Immigrant Deer" other elements necessary to realising these animals as natural history objects are documented. The script connects the editing and scene shifts to the narration and soundtrack. Narrated by Douglas Dorward, there is extensive elaboration of not just what the animals are doing on screen but why: "Antlers, for instance, are marks of rank, there's no doubt about who's superior when a mature stag approaches a young one."[25] Sometimes these narrations deploy the rhetoric of science and facts, at other times they are anthropomorphic: "It's a shoving match only, like a rugby scrum." Narration works to give the images authority, the disembodied sober male voice adding gravitas and credibility to the "objective" visual display. The soundtrack is a complex interplay of Dorwood's monologue, "natural sounds" and music. These post-production documents give insights into the television process, the divisions of labour and the layers of mediation involved. They also highlight the temporally extended and huge collective effort that was necessary to produce a natural history animal in the context of a public broadcaster. All provide powerful evidence of the elaborate amount of provocation and creative work involved.

This focus on construction, creativity and multiple mediators confirms our central argument that the natural history animal had to be provoked and crafted. In the shooting phase these provocations often sought to literally incite a response in animals, to trigger effects in their bodies, to bring them forth. The materiality of the animal body, its actions, its presence or absence, were potent forces in configuring

---

24 "Rather undisciplined rambling notes and ideas". ABC NHU Archive, Box 11/1427.
25 "Post Production Film Script – Wildlife of Papua New Guinea, The Immigrant Deer". Produced by David Parer. ABC NHU Archive, Box 11/1427.

3 Developing the natural history genre

and mediating the shoot. In subsequent production phases animal performances were worked over and layered with other elements – different sociotechnical processes, different mediators and different protocols about what made the emerging televisual natural history animal plausible and real.

Accounting for natural history animals: Science and art

Parer's field notes and the post-production documents about "The Immigrant Deer" signal the early development of the natural history genre in the ABC and the emergence of some of its key cultural conventions. The opening narration over aerial shots of the river and the vast plains with masses of grazing deer signals that a story is about to be told about, as the male voiceover notes: "one of the most extensive wetlands left in the world, a panorama of water and cloud". Nature and wildlife are initially introduced from a god's eye perspective: utterly separate, out there and sublime. As the program unfolds, this panoramic perspective is displaced with a "nature" that is grounded in a range of different points of view and narratives ranging from biology to environmental history to anthropology. The animals in this program are biological objects performing their wildness but also mixed up with human worlds, vulnerable and in need of management or conservation. Sometimes they are detached from humans in an ontology of essentialised natural difference; at other times they are attached in networks of interaction and negotiation. These diverse knowledges and points of view are deftly managed by the pedagogic and expository imperative of the narration. Information is offered with an explicitly instructional intent: viewers are given stories and explanations that direct how these visual animals are to be known.

These early conventions show how the meanings and modes of being of natural history animals start to differentiate them from other televisual animals. These differences are more than just stylistic; they are about the kinds of knowledges and assumptions that authorise these animals as credible, and the ways in which animals become implicated in other realities that are referenced as the source of this credibility. They are also about specific regimes of value, how the significance of these animals is established in ways that provoke particular human dispositions towards them and establish the cultural authority of the genre. As we have outlined, the natural history animal is often identified as emerging in the ecology of quality public service broadcasters, but what was it about this ecology that conferred special value on these animals? How were these animals accounted for so that they came to be seen as not only believable but as more authoritative and authentic than those screened on the commercial channels?

The idea of "accounting" for animals refers to situated practices of looking and telling. In filming animals, it wasn't enough to make them visible or observable, there also had to be various mechanisms established for holding these images to account as persuasive and definitive evidence of animal realities. Accountability is not about meaning but *how* images work.[26] While accountability relations were central to the development of the natural history genre, their most potent effect was the way they implicated the natural history animal in networks of power and possibility. A key way in which this was done was through the demarcation of subject and object, or seer and seen. Much of the visual framing and narration of natural history content established clear distinctions between humans as the subjects of knowledge and animals as the objects of this knowledge; it established fundamentally anthropocentric modes of viewing. This distinction established various relations between humans and animals. While anthropomorphic accounts of animals, for example, may have framed them in terms of their similarity with humans and allowed humans to identify with them, animals were still *other*: like us but different. Ultimately, animals were in the service of provoking and satisfying human interest and curiosity.

But what sorts of accounts shaped these animals and modes of viewing? As we saw in the previous chapter, televisual animals before the ascendancy of the NHU often drew on diverse knowledges to justify their screen realities. In the case of *Dancing Orpheus* (ABC, 1962), we saw that the lyrebird was primarily an aesthetic object. The visual references and narrative were explicitly high cultural, drawing on Greek mythology, classical music and notions of majestic natural expression

---

26 Neyland and Coopmans 2014.

3 Developing the natural history genre

that framed the bird as, above all else, beautiful. This technique enacted the ABC's authority as an institution for the cultural improvement of populations and invited audiences to adopt an aesthetic disposition towards the animals on display; it also prefigured the emergent natural history genre. While scientific knowledge was drawn on in *Dancing Orpheus*, it wasn't necessarily dominant; this information was mixed up with aesthetic framings in this mode of visualisation. These interactions between art and science implicitly referenced the long genealogy of "natural history" as a practice of closely observing and displaying nature in all its beauty and exotic diversity.

This aesthetic legacy in cultures of natural history was beautifully captured in a 1972 program under the badge "Wild Australia" called *Wild Australia: Beyond the Dunes* (ABC, 1972). This program featured well-known Australian artist John Olsen sketching waterbirds alongside a cameraman. Filming and sketching were presented as parallel methods for closely observing and representing birds, each with their specific technical possibilities and limits but also equally valid. In the on-air version the drawings from Olsen often dissolved into filmed images of the same bird, and vice versa. As Olsen said in an interview about the project: "It raises all sorts of questions – what is reality, what is film, what is drawing?"[27] In posing this question, the empirical authority of the camera was not privileged; there were diverse ways to observe and craft animal realities. One TV reviewer described Olsen's sketches in the program as "having an oriental simplicity, a sense of space ... a tiny bird on a twig with an enormous space about it, becomes a symbol of our existence".[28] In this evaluation, it was the capacity of artists to situate animals in wider human philosophical reflection that made their visualisations unique and implicitly superior to science. Another reviewer noted that she had never seen "such beauty, such splendid TV. It is a tribute to the men who waited patiently for hours, filming and painting."[29]

---

27 Laurie Thomas (1972). Spotlight on the untouched Australia. *Australian*, 16 May. ABC NHU Archive, Box 11/5779, no page numbers.
28 Laurie Thomas (1972). Spotlight on the untouched Australia. *Australian*, 16 May. ABC NHU Archive, Box 11/5779, no page numbers.

This early period of natural history programming, just before the NHU was officially established, appeared to have an ambivalent relation to science. When it came to accounting for animals, art and aesthetic approaches were often considered equally valuable for offering insights into the specificity and significance of animal modes of being. This is not to say that science was unimportant – after all, the narrator of *Beyond the Dunes* was Douglas Dorwood, a respected zoologist – rather that scientific methods were not privileged as the best or only way of observing and accounting for animals. As NHU producer at the time, Ken Taylor, noted, the challenge for NHU program makers was how to:

> give form to life's diversity, to seek wholeness beyond the steady observations of science. Film making without vision leads only to repetitive and listless formulae ... the old problem of reconciling art with science lies before us. The prospect that there can be a division between the two in natural history filmmaking is an illusion.[30]

He was right. As the NHU developed throughout the 1970s and began producing more and more content, art and science were more effectively reconciled as certain genre conventions solidified. Aestheticised animals gave way to more factual and entertaining ones. In this shift, scientific accounts of animals were reconfigured. Scientific knowledge was used not only to offer didactic lessons about animals to ignorant publics but also to promote and popularise science. Animals became enrolled as devices for representing scientific expertise, and for promoting the authority and public value of science. The rise of the natural history animal was pivotal in this process of popularising science.

These shifting and extended engagements with science took many different forms. During the 1970s and 1980s the NHU began seeking out funding and production partnerships with a range of scientific and environmental organisations. These partnerships weren't just driven

---

29 Nan Musgrove, Review of Beyond the Dunes. *The Australian Women's Weekly* (no date). ABC NHU Archive, Box 11/5779.
30 Taylor 1976.

by the chronic shortage of funds within the ABC for natural history productions, logistics was also a factor. Developing co-productions with various state and national scientific or conservation organisations gave the NHU access to experts, to remote places, and to research or conservation projects that had potential audience appeal. Throughout the 1970s and early 80s the NHU developed co-productions with, for example, the Victorian Forestry Commission (*Wildfire*, NHU, 1980), PNG Wildlife Division (*The Bird of the Thunderwoman*, NHU, 1980), the Great Barrier Reef Marine Park Authority (*Where Angels Swim*, NHU, 1981) and numerous other bodies. Often "scientists at work" was a major theme and focus of the programs. Animals and landscapes were framed as objects of research or conservation and scientists or park rangers their official spokespersons. In other examples, NHU programs reported new scientific discoveries about animals to audiences. According to Ken Taylor, the "Wild Australia" badged series reported the first scientific studies of species ranging from the Australian crane or brolga to surviving fur seal populations of Bass Strait.[31]

However, popularising science was also problematic. Not only could scientific knowledge be difficult to convey to mass audiences in an accessible way, scientific practices could be dull and unpredictable. Science had to be televisual and entertaining; it had to account for animals in ways that ensured they were fun to watch and not just informative. Scientific knowledge had to be reconciled with the expectations of the genre; it had to service and enhance those expectations, not undermine them. This didn't mean that science was completely constrained and disciplined by genre conventions. Rather, scientific knowledge and practices had to be adapted to develop the genre, to extend the possibilities of what could count as a credible and entertaining natural history animal on television. At the heart of this process was a negotiation between the demands of the medium and the authority of science, and animals and their unpredictability were often where these negotiations took place.[32]

---

31 Taylor 1976.
32 See Gouyon (2019), *BBC Wildlife Documentaries in the Age of Attenborough*, chapter 7, for an account of how the BBC's NHU dealt with science and scientists in its evolution.

Provoking entertaining animals

The third technique implicated in provoking natural history animals, beyond mediating and accounting, was making animals entertaining. As noted above, this was an expectation of the genre and it placed very particular demands on both animals and scientists. An example of how science was used to both account for animals and to render them entertaining was the program *The Man Who Loves Frogs* (ABC NHU, 1985), which showcased the work of scientist Michael Tyler, a leading researcher of Australian frogs. In 1982 Tyler, an academic in the Department of Zoology at Adelaide University, was approached by Dione Gilmour,[33] a director/producer in the NHU, to make a "frog film". Gilmour contacted Tyler after he had publicly criticised natural history shows as too fabricated. In taking up Gilmour's offer, Tyler agreed to a film crew following his research team as they went about collecting frogs in the wild. After discussions, it was decided to focus on unique Australian frogs and to foreground Tyler's passion for frogs and expertise, in order to give the program a "human interest angle".

Tyler described the selection of appropriate frogs to film like this:

> It seemed that if the film was to have appeal to audiences outside Australia, then it was good sense to film species with attributes not represented overseas. The gastric brooding frog was an obvious choice. So too was a fat little frog that lives in sand dunes in Shark Bay in Western Australia, emerging at night to feed on ants ... Locomotion, reproduction, adaptation to the arid environment ... and even the problems created by the introduced cane toad: all were needed to present an accurate and fascinating record of the frog fauna of Australia.[34]

---

33 Dione Gilmour worked in the ABC's NHU for almost 25 years. She has been described as the "doyenne of natural history television in Australia". While in the NHU she did researching, producing, directing and presenting and eventually became head of the unit for its last nine years. She was responsible for a huge number of award-winning natural history programs including the *Nature of Australia* series, which is examined in Chapter 5. https://realscreen.com/1998/08/01/22762-19980801/.

34 Frogs – a man and his obsession. *Look and Listen Magazine* 7 May 1985, 75.

3 Developing the natural history genre

This account beautifully captures the hybrid expectations of the "natural history frog". This frog had to appeal to audiences outside Australia in order to generate export sales and therefore economic value. It had to have entertainment value in the sense of being weird and visually interesting, and it had to have scientific value by offering a comprehensive and accurate record of the diversity of the species and its biological habits. Going on to explain the complexities and challenges of the actual film shoot, Tyler gave extensive descriptions of how difficult it was to make scientific frogs into natural history frogs. He writes like an alien in a strange world of bewildering protocols and practices. The demands of continuity, filming at night, not being able to look directly at the camera even when it was only a metre away – all these practices gave him renewed admiration for television production as an "art that we grew to respect and admire".[35]

But the most interesting aspect of his reflections relates to what happened to his scientific ethics and protocols when the film crew entered his laboratory to shoot close-ups of specific frog behaviours. Tyler notes how his: "admiration for the ABC crew, particularly their ingenuity, influenced our own attitudes".[36] He is referring to the fact that, after months of being around a film crew, he eventually became comfortable provoking scientific "facts" to happen on cue for the camera. He describes injecting female frogs with hormones so they would produce egg masses for the camera and giving burrowing frogs a sharp prod so they would emerge at just the right moment. In negotiations between the scientists and filmmakers about what to film and how, it was agreed that the animal body needed to be manipulated. Natural behaviours were going to be an effect of filming, not its passive object.

Tyler also reflects on how his scientific ethics were challenged and extended by the demands of the televisual. Interfering with animals, provoking them to perform on cue, didn't necessarily undermine scientific credibility, it helped enact it in this particular media ecology. Making the animal visual by manipulating it meant making it entertaining *and* communicable. In the context of using TV to

---

35 Frogs – a man and his obsession. *Look and Listen Magazine* 7 May 1985, 78.
36 Frogs – a man and his obsession. *Look and Listen Magazine* 7 May 1985, 78.

popularise science, this ethical imperative overrode others. For Tyler, the fact that the natural history film crew was able to capture superb close-ups of frogs, that it could, for example, generate remarkable slow motion footage of them landing after a huge leap, was of immense scientific *and* entertainment value. These were scientific facts made televisual that also revealed aspects of animal reality that had never been seen before by the naked eye and mass audiences, animal realities that only the techniques of filmmaking could produce.

While scientific knowledge and expertise were central to how these frogs were visualised and accounted for, this knowledge did not abstract the frogs as facts, or mere objects of knowledge. In the program, Tyler speaks about frogs as a scientist *and* a passionate enthusiast. He is "obsessed" with them, immersed in and attached to their worlds. Frogs make him, as much as he makes them. Science in this program was about affect and wonder not just expertise and objective knowledge. Tyler's difficult searches for new species, his delight and pleasure in encountering frogs in the wild, implicated the scientist's body and affections in the frogs and generated, for the audience, a sense of "being with" them and not just looking at them.

Manipulations of animals were common in Natural History Unit productions, as they were (and continue to be) in many televisual wildlife productions. The use of domesticated, imprinted or captive animals to simulate wild behaviours in highly controlled filming situations was standard practice. This got around the problem of waiting and hoping that animals would show up and perform. Making them perform, training them to perform, ensured that their "natural" reality could be displayed and publicly witnessed. In *The Man Who Loves Frogs* these practices were deployed, but what is interesting is how the scientist narrator justified them. It was not simply a question of the film crew encouraging Tyler to be "ingenious" in his relations with the laboratory frogs, it was also a question of Tyler *wanting* the frogs to be entertaining, to perform their unique behaviour, to be the scientific and televisual objects that authorised his knowledge as an expert and explained his deep attachment to them.

The use of scientific knowledge and scientists to account for the natural history animal became a powerful convention in the consolidation of the genre.[37] While there were different ways in which science and scientists were enrolled in these programs, there is no doubt that natural history content on the ABC helped popularise science and establish its authority as one of the most important and "objective" ways of knowing animals. Science appeared as uncontroversial and settled knowledge that was applicable to any animal or landscape. Television created a very particular world in which animals and scientists were related in new and interesting ways. The demands and logics of television placed significant demands on animals as "objects" of science and they also changed the character of science itself. Scientists weren't just detached experts, they were obsessed, affected and often passionate advocates and spokespersons for animals and their worlds.

The ways in which natural history animals were provoked, mediated and accounted for in NHU programs during the 1970s and 80s were diverse. As we have argued, these accounts functioned not so much to establish what the images meant but *how* they meant, how they could be understood as credible evidence of specific animal ontologies. They also gave shape to the natural history genre and helped establish its cultural authority. What was critical about accounting for animals as natural history beings was the way in which aesthetic dimensions interacted with scientific dimensions. Animals were displayed as spectacular, beautiful and fascinating, and as embodiments of remarkable facts and fascinating behaviours that often only a scientist or naturalist could truly understand and communicate. These accounts reference a long cultural tradition of natural history display with its emphasis on public spectacle and public demonstration. They also shaped audience modes of viewing and experiencing animals in very particular ways. The idea that animals were there to be displayed *for* humans fuelled the anthropocentricism of TV representations. According to Eleanor Louson (2018), what televisual natural history shows often provoke are the dual effects of scopophilia and epistemophilia: pleasure in seeing animal spectacle *and* simultaneously accessing knowledge about those animals; pleasure in showing *and* telling.[38] The effect of these practices and genre conventions was that

---

37 Gouyon 2019.
38 Louson 2018.

natural history animals were provoked into the service of acquisitive human pleasures, there to be observed and known and to be entertaining and informative. Being too controversial or confronting threatened human expectations and pleasures. Natural history animals had to know their place.

4
Making-of documentaries
Turning working animals into natural history animals

The provocations and production practices used to craft natural history animals on the ABC during the 1970s and 80s were unseen by the audience. While these provocations were central to making animals that realised the codes and conventions of the genre, they were generally backstaged. The effect of this concealment was to reassure viewers that the origin of the animals represented on screen was nature, not the television apparatus. Gradually, as the genre became more sophisticated and its production techniques more complex, it was obvious that the type of vision made available on natural history TV was elaborately technically enhanced and manipulated. The animals on display were not unobtrusively observed, they were made for television. This shift in the presence and power of the medium to bring animals close, to reveal aspects of them that had never been seen before, to render them knowable, spectacular and pleasurable, recognised the technogenesis of the natural history animal – its fundamental dependence on technologies of vision to call it into being.

A significant development in this shift was the rise of the making-of documentary (MOD) that went behind the scenes of wildlife production and revealed the televisual apparatus in action. Far from concealing filmmaking tricks and techniques, these programs celebrated them. They are symptomatic of what Jan Teurlings describes as the rise of "the society of the machinery", or a major mutation in popular culture in which the self-evidence of representations is debunked and audiences are invited to look beyond appearances and engage with the technical and organisational aspects of media production.[1]

In this chapter we focus on one fascinating and paradigmatic MOD from the 2015 Sky TV series *David Attenborough's Conquest of the Skies* (Atlantic Productions, 2014),[2] which explored the evolution of flight. In a fourth episode, screened after the three official episodes, the production techniques used to make the series were examined. This episode was called "The Making of David Attenborough's Conquest of the Skies" (Colossus Productions, 2014)[3] and was promoted as offering rare insights into how wildlife or natural history television was made. This MOD manifests all the standard conventions of the format. It emerges from an (unseen) film crew following and filming the official film crew and revealing the machinery and mess of television production practices, introducing crew members and explaining their professional roles and showing animals "backstage" with their handlers being wrangled. The episode operates in the "reflexive mode" of documentary. It uses many of the same devices as standard documentary but "sets them on edge so that the viewer's attention is drawn to the device as well as the effect".[4] This reflexive mode is, of course, never-ending.

When it comes to MODs about natural history television, there has been limited analysis. Richard Kilborn and John Izod dismiss them as cynical attempts to extend the profitability of the content, to extract more value by having a documentary crew follow the official TV crew and expose the secrets of television.[5] They have also been critiqued as examples of the acquisitive and predatory nature of wildlife TV, as

---

1 Teurlings 2013, 518.
2 *David Attenborough's Conquest of the Skies* series was directed by David Lee for Atlantic Productions, one of the world's leading factual and multi-platform production companies.
3 "The Making of David Attenborough's Conquest of the Skies" episode was directed by Edward McGown for Colossus Productions. See http://tinyurl.com/ya95ft7p.
4 Nichols 1991, 33.
5 Kilborn and Izod 1997.

4 Making-of documentaries

further evidence of the format's insatiable appetite for revealing more and more aspects of animal being.[6] These assessments are significant and politically astute, but they ignore a critical element: the dynamics of revelation and reflexivity or the interactions between the official series and the "see all" documentary over what counts as "real". Our interest in this MOD is in how it discloses some of the processes involved in provoking animals to perform for television, how a domesticated animal becomes a natural history animal and the implications of this for the official series.

This is not to claim that this "Making of" episode offers unproblematic access to what really happens behind the official representation, far from it. MODs are still representations, highly constructed and selective in terms of what they reveal and conceal. The issue is how they operate in dialogue with the official series and how they produce very different animal realities. These programs celebrate the dynamics of staging and the ingenuity of media production processes in getting animals to perform their natural selves or scientific facts.[7] More critically, the accountability relations that are devised to authorise these behind-the-scenes animal realities, to make them compelling and convincing, to generate the effect of seeing the working animal behind the natural history animal, are very different to those developed in the official series. And it is this difference, between how natural history and backstage working animals are *made real*,[8] that generates fascinating insights into the ways in which diverse animal realities are provoked and done rather than found and represented.

This approach to "doing reality" challenges many of the assumptions underpinning existing investigations of wildlife TV and screen animals more generally. It foregrounds the diverse processes involved in crafting realistic screen animals. For Anat Pick, realism is ineluctably material; it involves a dense web of material, social and technical associations that inscribe the world in a cinematic or televisual habitat.[9] For her, "realism, like reality, is a construction and

---

6   Cubitt 2005; Pick and Narraway 2013.
7   Gouyon 2016.
8   Michael 2017; Mol 1999.
9   Pick 2015a.

a point of view that denotes a mode of involvement".[10] This materialist orientation to how a screen reality is called forth and how it implicates and involves audiences sets Pick apart from many analyses of wildlife media that remain trapped in representational thinking or ideology critique. It also resonates with science and technology (STS) approaches that understand reality in surprisingly similar ways: as crafted, as emerging from interactions between the world, modes of capturing or observing it and observers. For both Pick and STS, the outcomes of these interactions are not so much "social constructions" or "representations", but enactments that are highly manipulated but also ineluctably real.

Despite these conceptual resonances, however, there has been surprisingly little conversation between STS and media or screen studies. MODs present an interesting opportunity to productively extend this dialogue to questions of how media realities are done. The empirical test for both fields is to document the contingent elements and mechanisms that become practically operative in making a reality: to examine the specific material, technical, cultural and institutional dynamics that are endowed with constructive capacities in distinct settings. In taking up Pick's arguments and recent debates in STS, we want to develop a different orientation to the fact that televisual animals are simulated and contrived. By focusing on how the birds in *Conquest of the Skies* are practically *made real*, our aim is to shift from a representational idiom to a performative one.[11] Rather than evaluate the adequacy of animal representations in relation to an essentialised animal reality, the aim of this chapter is to investigate *how* televisual animals emerge as contingent outcomes of the manner in which they are both provoked and staged. We also want to understand how these animal realities and performances become capable of shaping distinct animal–human relations and contact zones.

---

10   Pick 2015a, 224.
11   Muniesa 2014, 10.

4 Making-of documentaries

Provoking realities: A brief conceptual foray

"The Making of David Attenborough's Conquest of the Skies" (Colossus Productions, 2014) is a visual representation, but its reflexive mode, its commitment to revelation, continually foregrounds the technical and material organisation of representations, the way in which they emerge from myriad human, animal and nonhuman elements and relations. This reflexivity disrupts the tendency towards interpretation and the idea of visual representations as a surface or static text on which hidden ideologies are projected.[12] Instead, the viewer is positioned in a post-representational mode[13] that foregrounds how images are composed and how they are accounted for or made credible. In this MOD, audiences see domesticated animals that are provoked to perform rather than captured in a state of "nature" that is the reality effect of the official episodes.[14] In one particular sequence that we investigate in detail, we see whooper swans arrive in the back of a mini-van with their owner/trainer, then being released onto the edge of a lake surrounded by film crew and handlers. During the shoot the swans are encouraged to fly in formation across the lake so that the aerodynamics of flight can be captured in close-up. These swans are working animals and performers. On the film set they are incited to demonstrate their natural capacities in order to make a scientific fact both visible and televisually spectacular.

Inciting, crafting and provoking are the terms that underpin our analysis. These terms refuse essentialism and highlight the dynamics of ontological enactment. While they have similar connotations, and are often used interchangeably, they also have particular nuances and emphases. As discussed in the previous chapter, provoking is our preferred conceptual tool. In our assessment, the idea of *provoking* reality gets closest to the distinct practices that were involved in making animals televisual for the ABC's NHU. In relation to the MOD under examination in this chapter, the concept gains even greater traction as

---

12 Lorimer 2015; Lynch 2005.
13 Lorimer 2010; Thrift 2007.
14 Hawkins and Dibley 2020.

it is, quite literally, what happens to these whooper swans. They arrive on set and are coaxed and provoked into displaying certain behaviours.

Recent work by Muniesa[15] and Lezaun, Muniesa and Vikkelsø[16] has explored the idea of provocation as a distinct reality-generating practice. In one line of analysis Lezaun and colleagues use the term "provocative containment" to scrutinise a specific type of, now discredited, social scientific experiment in which various interventions and devices were deployed in very restricted and controlled settings in order to stimulate a response in participants that could be observed. As Lezaun and colleagues put it: "Provocative containment is thus a technique for the production and display of social reality. Provocation is to be understood here in the sense of both generation and challenge. To provoke is to trigger an effect."[17] They go on to argue that "provoked" realities involve practices that produce "vivid and otherwise unavailable renderings of social reality".[18]

Provocative containment, then, is a technique that produces a very particular sort of reality. For Lezaun and colleagues, these experimental practices were not driven by the desire to reveal social phenomenon available elsewhere. Rather, their aim was to manipulate, demonstrate and render explicit a reality that is largely an effect of acts of provocation and intervention. The realities that emerged from experiments in provocative containment could be described as representations. They were manipulations of the world in order to generate real social phenomenon. While Lezaun and colleagues accept critiques of these realities as contrived and fabricated, their analytic purpose is not to adjudicate on whether such practices produce effective knowledge or are ethical. Rather, they are interested in *how* these experiments brought into existence something that otherwise would not have happened. The conditions prompting the behaviours under observation might have been highly artificial and contained, but the performances were very real. The term they use to describe this paradox is "factitious".[19] This

---

15 Muniesa 2014.
16 Lezaun, Muniesa and Vikkelsø 2013.
17 Lezaun, Muniesa and Vikkelsø 2013, 279.
18 Lezaun, Muniesa and Vikkelsø 2013, 280.
19 Lezaun, Muniesa and Vikkelsø 2013, 279.

framing of the real and how it is stimulated makes the concept of "provocative containment" very suggestive for investigating how animal realities are generated for television.

Provocation challenges the idea that the formless objectivity of animals awaits visual capture that will lay bare their singular and authentic reality. Instead, it foregrounds the myriad processes whereby a reality emerges as an effect of various incitements and devices.[20] It draws attention to the processes of both stimulating *and* crafting animal realities, and the effects of broadcasting and circulating them. It also foregrounds the event and interactivity of provocation as a reality-generating technique, and the ways in which it involves both an interventionist *and* a reactive relation to the world. The idea of a genuine unconfined empirical reality collapses in this framework, as do concerns with representational correspondence or accuracy. Instead, questions about the specific techniques and practices of media provocations become central, particularly how the world pushes back and how animal bodies and agencies are registered and negotiated.

This account of provocation resonates with Pick's explorations of the nature of cinematic realism. Specifically, how the ecologies of cinema generate particular material and sociotechnical relationships between the medium and animal worlds. A central concern for Pick is how the reality of the world and the realism of the medium are mutually enabled and enacted.[21] Like Muniesa, Pick understands reality and realism beyond positivist and essentialist registers and beyond notions of strict indexicality. In an analysis that resonates with STS without explicitly referencing it, she explains:

> The world is not "out there" to be captured by mechanical means. Reality is always artificial, or virtual, insofar as it is crafted between subject and object, not an entity but a *procedure*: the creative process of "showing forth" coauthored by subject and object. Understood in this way, realism designates an overcoming of the subject/object divide by alluding to a seamless continuum.[22]

---

20 Muniesa 2014, 21.
21 Pick 2015a.
22 Pick 2015a, 224 (our emphasis).

Muniesa and Pick are on the same page: realities are multiple, they are provoked and crafted, they are real. However, there are also important differences. Muniesa's investigations of contained experiments and the dynamics of provocation focus on the epistemic power of these techniques, how they established the authority of what unfolded as valid and real; engineered but also authentic. Pick analyses similar issues about the cinematic *dispositif* and its ability to assemble believable worlds, but she is also interested in the political effects of these realities, the implications of particular animal ontologies on screen. For her, it is not simply a question of how animal realities are done, how they perform, but for whom and with what consequences? How might these realities provoke ethical or political concerns about animal–human relations? In pursuing this issue, Pick has explored the possibilities of "zoomorphic realism", specifically the capacity of cinema to frame animal lifeworlds. If animals have *umwelts*, or lifeworlds, then media may provoke or craft these in ways that allow "the possibility of really entering and understanding other lives".[23] To be captured by zoomorphic realism on screen – or the sense of inhabiting an animal perspective and *umwelt* – involves an inevitable displacement of anthropocentrism, and it is this radical potential that signals Pick's concern not simply with *how* realities are done but their ethico-political force and implications.[24]

In shifting from notions of representation to provocation, the focus in what follows is how working animals in this MOD are provoked into becoming natural history animals and the specific forms of accountability that establish these different animal performances as real. We are also interested in how these realities generate particular modes of involvement and affects in audiences. While television content is our primary empirical material, we approach this not as a discrete domain of visual representation, not as a text awaiting critical

---

23 Pick 2015a, 227.
24 Brett Mills' (2010) discussion of the notion of the animal's right to privacy in the context of wildlife documentary further complicates the politics of "zoomorphic realism" (Pick 2015a), since an implication of his argument suggests that the cinematic apparatus should be constrained with regard to its penetration of the animals' *umwelt*.

readings but as material that *realises* animals, that configures an observed animal reality and an observer through myriad practices and sociotechnical devices. The question is: How does this MOD both contain animals and reveal new realities about them? And what ethical and political concerns might these televisual animals generate?

Whooper swans at work

The *David Attenborough's Conquest of the Skies* (Atlantic Productions, 2014) series explored the evolution of flight and the technical achievements of, as the promotional blurb put it, "nature's greatest aeronauts". Shot in 3D, it was screened around the world on streaming and free-to-air channels. The extensive global sales of this program are evidence of both audience demand for spectacular animal content and the power of the brand that is David Attenborough. The MOD on the series was filmed and directed by Edward McGown. It was screened at the end and promoted as a fourth episode. The format of the MOD involved revisiting key scenes in the series and showing the production processes and technical innovations involved in creating them. "Making-of" content, while not always a full episode, is now a standard component of many natural history documentaries and is regularly included in DVD and web releases. As noted, critics of this content often dismiss it as driven by profit and offering little more than promotional celebrations of new camera technologies or the patience and tenacity of the heroic filmmaker. As Kilborn and Izod point out, "we are told remarkably little about other aspects of the production, including the funding arrangements or the editing process".[25] This critique stands for "The Making of David Attenborough's Conquest of the Skies" (Atlantic Productions, 2014).

While there is no question that one of the key functions of MODs is to extend the economic value of the content by exploiting audience fascination with the actual processes of getting animals on screen, they have other effects. According to Pick and Narraway, this audience fascination is partially an effect of what they call the increasing "ocular

---

25 Kilborn and Izod 1997, 225.

inflation" of the wildlife genre; that is, a desire and expectation to see nature and animals in ways that involve heightened visibility or forms of seeing that are extensive and acquisitive.[26] This ocular inflation is often framed in terms of "never before seen footage" that is celebrated as a technical feat delivering vision beyond the capacity of a normal human gaze. In this way, the televisual animal emerges as fundamentally technical, as only coming into being *in relationship* with various technologies and devices.[27]

Like most MODs, "The Making of David Attenborough's Conquest of the Skies" is predicated on a logic of disclosure and revelation, its appeal is based on appearing to get beyond the surface of representations. However, just like the official episodes, it is highly constructed with specific codes about what gets disclosed and what remains concealed or left out. For Gouyon, the purpose of revelation in wildlife MODs is to reinforce the scientific authority of the official series.[28] This often means explaining how natural facts are reconstructed for television. The MOD addresses the audience as savvy viewers who understand that wildlife content involves performances of nature and science and sets out to show how these performances are realised.

The scene of particular relevance to our argument shows how one of the penultimate and most promoted scenes of the official series, whooper swans (*Cygnus cygnus*) flying over Loch Lomond, was created. In the official series, Attenborough is shown speeding along in a boat as four swans fly in perfect formation next to him. As they fly, he explains the aerodynamics of flight to the audience. The camera moves between the celebrity narrator speaking to the audience, intense close-ups of the birds' wings and chests flying just above him, and the majestic landscape. The birds are mediated and authorised by Attenborough; his narration constitutes them as scientific and aesthetic wonders. The swan performances are spectacular and appear to be perfectly disciplined for the wildlife genre and its promise to show animals being their remarkable natural selves.

---

26 Pick and Narraway 2013, 21; see also Pick 2015b.
27 This resonates with Braun and Whatmore's (2010) account of technogenesis and Haraway's (2008) analysis of National Geographic's *Crittercam* series.
28 Gouyon 2016.

In the MOD, this scene is one of several that are explored through a reflexive conversation built on constant intercutting between the official sequence that went to air and the behind-the-scenes processes of creating it. The MOD shows two animal realities: the working animal being coaxed into performing as a natural history animal. While these animals inhabit the same body, they are accounted for in very different ways. In the "Making of" episode, the whooper swans are revealed as participants in the production process; the provocation techniques of filming have to negotiate with and contain their distinct and unpredictable animal modes of being. This episode reveals and acknowledges the swans' agency, something that is elided in the official series where they are reduced to natural history animals displaying their incredible physical capacities. In the "Making of" scene, the swans are not authorised through Attenborough, instead they are shown as present and potent participants that are being provoked by *and are also provoking* the televisual apparatus. By the time these swans get to the official series, they have become reconfigured as objects of natural wonder and scientific fact. However, before that, they are animal subjects with histories and working lives.

The "Making of" scene begins with the director of the series, David Lee, outlining the purpose of the swan sequence direct to camera. The aim of the scene, he says, is to show swans flying very close to David Attenborough so that he can explain the complex aerodynamics of flight: "It should be amazing on 3D camera!" Lee enthuses. Meanwhile, in the background, four whooper swans wander nonchalantly out of a large white van, down a ramp and into the foreground. The animal talent has arrived. Then the swans' "mother" is introduced. She is Rose Buck, a bird specialist. Buck is seen petting the swans and calling them down to the edge of the loch with whoop whoop noises; she is becoming a whooper swan at the same time as the swans seem remarkably comfortable on the set. Then Buck speaks directly to camera, describing the swans' infancy and how they imprinted with her. We see snapshots of the swans as cygnets tucked up in bed with Buck, swimming with her, being fed by her. The narrator explains that these cosy domestic images show that "the swans believe that Buck is their mother and will follow her anywhere" and it is this unique human–animal relationship that underpins the scene. The narrator goes on to explain that the official scene would have been impossible without swans that were domesticated and imprinted on Buck, as it was her calling them that encouraged them to fly so close to the boat and the camera.

The next scene moves to the edge of the lake to a large speedboat laden with crew and equipment. The complex technologies of filmmaking are shown, and at the heart of it all is what the narrator describes as the "heavy, specially stabilised 3D camera equipment". There is lots of observational footage of blokey discussion between the crew about boats, filmmaking devices, uncertain weather conditions and close-ups of the camera being adjusted. The huge 3D camera is established as a major actant. In Latour and Woolgar's terms, it is an inscription device, something that will make the enactment and circulation of this reality possible.[29]

In the "Making of" sequence we see how much is invested in getting the swan scene right; it is explained as the linchpin for the whole series. The imperative in showing the aerodynamics of swan flight is not just to explain a scientific fact but also to make an extraordinarily spectacular visual sequence for the series, a "money shot". Constant references to the necessity of getting great footage authorise all this effort and highlight the way in which the swans' flight is not being documented but actively provoked. When all is ready, the boat heads out into the loch with Attenborough and Buck up front accompanied by a rousing soundtrack. It is travelling to the release point for the swans. The narrator explains that in the official sequence all that will be seen is Attenborough and the swans. Buck will be out of shot. When the boat gets close to the swans standing on shore, Buck stands up in the boat, cups her hands to her mouth and begins calling them. The swans quickly take flight, following the boat and Buck's whoops, and the 3D camera begins to film. All is going well until suddenly the swans veer off course and return to the shore. Cut to an exasperated crew and Attenborough shaking his head in disappointment. Take two begins. Once again the swans start well, flying next to the boat and focused on Buck, with the camera zooming in close to their bodies and wings. Then the narrator explains that trouble is brewing because the weather

---

29   Latour and Woolgar 1986.

4 Making-of documentaries

is closing in. Will they be able to finish filming the scene before a huge storm breaks? Will the swans stay on course and stop veering out of shot? Attenborough also chips in, offering sympathy for the swans and explaining that "they're doing their best, but they don't necessarily understand where they need to be for the camera".

These invitations to the audience to feel both sympathy for the swans and crew and suspense about whether the scene will be realised are very effective. The swans are getting tired and possibly confused. The film crew is freezing and frustrated with the difficulty of the conditions and the swans' unpredictability. However, what is most powerful in this scene is the way it reveals various worlds not awaiting representation but *interacting*. The force of the scene is in watching a multiplicity of realities rubbing up against one another: the filmmaking apparatus, the swans, the weather, the humans; all are relating and affecting one another. A reality is being *done* here; it is being provoked and called forth, not passively apprehended. As you watch the "Making of" sequence, you have a strong sense of a televisual whooper swan reality emerging rather than being discovered and observed.

Accounting for realities

The reflexive mode of "The Making of David Attenborough's Conquest of the Skies" (Atlantic Productions, 2014) is built on both interrogating and enhancing the natural history authority of the animal realities screened in the official series. The MOD interrogates the official series by revealing that direct observation of nature is a fantasy, at the same time as it enhances the scientific validity of the animal performances by showing how facts are staged for television.[30] Seeing the swans contained by the filmmaking apparatus with its vans, cameras and handlers, and provoked into performing, involves far more than exposé and assumptions about getting to the true or concrete reality hiding behind the TV reality. Instead, the MOD makes different images available to the audience and establishes a completely different set of accountability relations for them. These images provide visual evidence

---

30 Gouyon 2016.

of the complexities of filmmaking with domesticated animals and the processes of crafting a televisual reality. The official series displays evidence of the swan's aeronautical capacities. Questions of veracity or correspondence are not at stake here; rather, it is the way in which different animal realities are practically generated and accounted for that matters.

For Neyland and Coopmans, making things visible depends on accountable ways of questioning vision or establishing "the practical arrangements in which visible evidence becomes (or is inhibited from being) subject to *interrogation*".[31] There is no doubt that the MOD is driven by a logic of interrogation. The question that it generates in audiences is: How did they do that? How did they get those swans to perform in that way? This is established as "what counts" in this episode, what shapes its structure, what needs to be revealed. Showing the swans' social history and domestic life and explaining the process of imprinting provides one answer, but so too does the focus on the technical devices and cultural protocols involved in the shoot. Also significant are the accounts of the setting and how variables such as the weather and fading light become participants in the process. This interrogative technique implicates the audience in the accountability relations of the program. They are shown aspects of how a televisual animal is constructed and are invited into the contingencies and dynamics of crafting a reality.

These more distributed and interrogative accountability relations in the MOD are completely excluded from the official natural history series. In the official episodes the evidentiary authority of the visual images is established not simply by concealing all the mess of filmmaking but by deploying standard genre codes and by amplifying the power of Attenborough, the trustworthy and commanding narrator. Attenborough speaks *for* the swans and *about* them. Using various forms of knowledge ranging from biology to physics, he authorises their natural realities as fixed and stable. With the help of television, Attenborough appears to make a pre-given wild reality knowable and accessible. The effect of this expository style of narration is to inhibit any sort of interrogative dynamic. Attenborough and scientific facts

---

31   Neyland and Coopmans 2014, 2 (emphasis in original).

establish the evidential certainty of the visual images and ensure that it is not open to question. The audience is here to learn, to be informed and entertained. In the MOD, accountability is decentred and redistributed. Not only is the audience invited to ask questions about the swans, the swans themselves are afforded certain forms of agency to account for themselves. Their infancy, their intimate relationship with Buck, their negotiations with the huge apparatus that is the film crew, reveal the "natural" or "wild" reality in the official series as very partial. These swans have *many* realities. This pluralisation of animal realities has a powerful amplificatory force. The MOD does not undermine the official reality, it offers a more complex explanation of how it is composed. As Alex Wilkie notes: "Constructivism ... does not aim to debunk, demystify or deflate but rather strengthen the production of knowledge claims by actively acknowledging the practices and techniques by which knowledge comes into being."[32]

Another significant effect of the reflexive mode of the MOD is the way that it offers a fascinating account of the role of the camera. The episode devotes a fair amount of attention to the 3D camera, which is celebrated for its technical capacity to visualise animals in new and remarkable ways. The audience is informed that it is a 3D camera offering incredible new forms of vision, that it is huge and expensive and requires excessive stabilisation; there are also lots of shots of the crew adjusting the camera and discussing its complexities. This content amplifies the role and authority of the camera in giving audiences access to "heightened visibility".[33] It also foregrounds the camera as a critical sociotechnical site of mediation and a key actant in making a televisual whooper swan reality. However, what is more important in the MOD is the way that the camera is framed as provoking rather than capturing a reality.

The shooting starts when the camera is finally ready and the swans are activated *by* the camera rolling and Buck's calls. The artistry and craft of TV production are also referenced as the structure of the scene and the critical position of the camera are carefully explained to the audience. Recognising the camera's power to trigger or stimulate

---

32   Wilkie 2018, 348.
33   Pick and Narraway 2013.

animal actions disrupts the idea that it mechanistically stands between an independent noumenal world and a perceiving human. Rather, the camera is revealed as both provocative *and* reactive. The camera activates a reality as it reaches into it; its technological capacity to record is mediated by preconceived commitments to particular angles and points of view that may be in the operator's mind or in the cultural conventions governing the genre. At the same time, the swans "don't necessarily understand where they need to be for the camera" (as Attenborough says on screen), so the camera has to react to and adapt to their actions. The camera is not reflecting or representing an enclosed natural world but is actively engaging with, intervening in and producing it.[34] Across all these relations and interfaces, a visual reality is called forth and crafted: a reality that Pick explains is a "more-than-subjective projection" that is determinedly situated in the real.[35]

Accounting for the TV camera as a provocation device, as the MOD does, also draws attention to the event of media production. The episode shows the contingency of the TV production process, the incredible logistics involved in setting up a shoot and the fragility of these arrangements. In STS, "events" refer to the compositional processes of making things happen. In events, heterogeneous elements – human and nonhuman, technical and cultural – interact and mutually affect one another and have their identities transformed in the process.[36] A persistent focus in STS has been on the performative dimensions of the research event or the scientific experiment: on the ways in which these activities are always interventions in the world that involve elaborate forms of co-fabrication and collaboration between the researcher and the researched as the world pushes back and affects, and is affected by, attempts to know it.[37] This understanding of research as eventful disrupts the opposition between the real and the constructed, or fact and fiction, and shows them to be synonymous in the processes of mapping things into knowledge.

---

34   Lynch 2005.
35   Pick 2015a, 222.
36   Michael 2017, 134.
37   Stengers 2008; Wilkie 2018.

The "factual" or natural history TV production could be considered in the same way: as an event that is compositional, that makes things happen and that develops specific accounts or framings of what is generated in order to establish its plausibility. The point is that to configure media production as an event or provocation draws attention to the material and sociotechnical dynamics of putting numerous elements into relation and investigating how these elements affect and constitute one another and enact a reality. It involves a commitment to documenting what the *realisation* of a media reality entails beyond empirical descriptions of the production process or investigations of economic imperatives or human intentions. It also highlights the material presence and potency of *animals* as active participants in shaping a televisual reality, and this is the issue we turn to next.

More-than-human publics: Provoking affective attunement

Probably the most important element in this sequence is the performance of the swans. In the official series the loch scene is used to explain aerodynamics; there is no reference to imprinting and no evidence of Rose Buck at the front of the boat calling the swans and activating their performance. She is completely excised. In the MOD the scientific narrative focuses on animal imprinting, hence the need to reveal Buck. In her role, Buck is heir to the ethologist, Konrad Lorenz, whose work with greylag geese (*Anser anser*) established the principles of imprinting. His research was documented in the 1937 film, *The Ethology of the Greylag Goose* (*Die Ethologie der Graugans*; Dir. Lorenz, Institut für den Wissenschaftlichen Film).[38] In this film there is footage of the scientist hailing his imprinted birds before paddling a boat and swimming in their company. In a sense, the sequence we are discussing is the hi-tech remake of Lorenz's film, but here domestication and imprinting are revealed and celebrated because they make the visualisation of a scientific fact and wildlife television possible.[39] In our analysis, domestication and imprinting could also be considered as

---

38 See Mitman (2009) for a discussion of this film.

forms of *sociobiological containment* that make the provocation of this televisual swan reality possible. But it is never a complete containment. As we see in the first attempt at filming the scene, the birds start well and then suddenly veer off course and out of shot. In the attempts to get the scene right, the swans propose to the film crew a very distinct manner of becoming together. They are very potent forces in this event. Provoking them requires careful human and nonhuman choreography. Everyone in the production team is attuned to the swans and so too are the technical devices, from the huge camera to the boat; all are adjusting their actions in relation to the swans. They are also attentive to many other things like the weather and the light, but the swans, more than anything else, organise everyone's attention and expectations. Everything is being altered in relation to the swans. In Vinciane Despret's framework, the swans are "articulating the system".[40] The swans are being provoked but they are also powerful provocateurs.

According to Despret, this complex dynamic is evidence of attunement, or relations of *mutual expectation* between humans and animals; it is about an openness to one another. As she says, "both are active and both are transformed by availability to the other".[41] In the "Making of" sequence we see the swans adjusting their bodies to the speed of the boat, and the wind and, most importantly, the call of Buck, their trainer/mother – they are affected by her body, as she is by theirs. Attunement is about how affect shapes bodies, how it moves them literally and emotionally. Affect doesn't emerge from the feeling subject, it is what makes a body, human or animal, responsive to the other and the world. Attunement is a form of mutual provocation.

In the official scene this relation of human–animal attunement is not disclosed. The swans' reality is authorised by Attenborough and the

---

39 The use of domesticated animals pretending to be wild has been central to the evolution of natural history film. The technical demands for such practices, the requirements of the close-up and questions of authenticity that they raise, have long been the subject of critical attention. See Bousé (2000) for a discussion along with a careful documentation of the abuses and indignities suffered by particular animals subjected to such film production regimes. Also see Gouyon (2016).
40 Despret 2004, 124.
41 Despret 2004, 125.

4 Making-of documentaries

voice of science and facts, but also by aesthetic regimes that render them spectacularly "natural" and beautiful by focusing closely on the animal body in flight.[42] These sociotechnical and genre devices *contain and objectify the swans*; they configure them as representative birds of televisual and scientific interest. In the MOD the swans' complex modes of being and performance are documented and acknowledged in many different ways beyond flight and their corporeality – walking out of the van, family snapshots of their early life in bed with Buck, flying off when they aren't meant to. We see the material and creative push of the animal body, its containment and its resistance; and we see the technical inventiveness of filmmaking as both responding to the animal and mediating it in order to create a televisual reality.

The "Making of" footage also invites the audience into the relationships of attunement that are documented on screen and creates a potent multispecies contact zone. In Despret's argument, attunement is different from empathy. Empathy makes the viewing subject feel, but it doesn't change the object of those feelings; it doesn't allow the object of empathy to be activated as a subject. In the MOD the swans are subjects, not just because we see their domestic life or because we see them as working animals but because we witness their availability, their openness to humans. We see what it is for them to be with the other, we see their distinctive reality as a product of relations that are natural *and* social *and* technical. And this calls an affective community into being that is *more than human*; a community that includes the swans as affecting and affected strangers that the audience is connected to, that they feel a form of "stranger sociability" with.[43]

In the MOD the whooper swans emerge as both provoked by and as provocateurs of the televisual *dispositif*. This sequence is especially powerful because it shows multiple animal realities: how the swans shift from natural objects of scientific wonder to key participants in a television production ecology. These swans have subjectivity, not just by anthropomorphising techniques or imprinting on a human but by their unique manners of being, their material and agentic capacities

---

42 This scrutiny of birds' bodies continues a long fascination with the animal body in the history of cinema (see Pick 2007).
43 Warner 2002, 74.

that affect both the crew and the audience. We see their realities as birds with a family history, as working animals struggling with tough weather conditions and repeated demands to perform. We see things from the animal point of view. While this may not be zoomorphic realism in Pick's sense,[44] it is perhaps getting close? In the official series, humans are firmly in control; the swans are there to be looked at as natural history animals. But in the realities made present in the MOD, the swans are encountered as animal workers and strangers that audiences feel affectively and ethically attuned to.

Conclusion

Provocation is a more complex concept than "staging" because it acknowledges the agency of animals in filmmaking practices and ecologies. While animals may be provoked into being their "natural" selves for television, they are also potent provocateurs. Provocation also alludes to the idea of filmmaking as an event, as an intervention in the world designed to make things happen. Finally, this concept is where STS and screen studies converge. In the work of Muniesa, Lezaun and Pick,[45] significant resonances emerge in their approaches to how realities are enacted or called forth, how they are mediated and how they are accounted for as real and credible.

The value of the "Making of" episode of *David Attenborough's Conquest of the Skies* (Atlantic Productions, 2014) is that it reveals some of the complex logistics involved in provoking animals to become natural history spectacles. In selecting this case, we did not see it as offering unproblematic or direct access to what really happens behind the scenes in wildlife TV production. Instead, our claim is that MODs are yet another subgenre or format driven by very specific conventions about what should be revealed, what is left out and why. Not only are these conventions very different from those deployed in official episodes, they are also in constant reflexive dialogue with them. This reflexive conversation between the two formats offers valuable insights

---

44   Pick 2015a.
45   Lezaun, Muniesa and Vikkelsø 2013; Muniesa 2014; Pick 2015a.

into two different whooper swan realities and how they are provoked. Neither is more real than the other. The whooper swans in the MOD are not more authentic; rather, they emerge as the effect of *different* provocations and different accountability relations. The MOD also reveals some of the mess and contingencies of natural history TV production as an event, as a compositional process of assembling a reality rather than observing one. Various heterogeneous elements – human and animal, technical and cultural combine – mutually affect one another, and have their identities transformed in the process. The camera is also visible and potent as a critical device for provoking and inscribing this reality. Unlike the official series, the camera has a presence and an identity and, by showing this, the effect of a natural animal reality observed from god's or Attenborough's point of view (basically the same thing) is disrupted. There is plenty that the MOD leaves out – it is still television after all. It is still driven by a commitment to entertain, to generate suspense, to invite various forms of public engagement with animals. It is just that the animals in the "Making of" episode are provoked as working creatures and the ones in the official episode as natural and spectacular.

Making these whooper swans real involves making sense of them at the same time, authorising their performances as credible evidence of what a swan is. Science is central here. In both sequences it plays a critical role. In the official sequence the aerodynamics of flight is used to frame the birds as extraordinary athletes, in the "Making of" sequence descriptions of imprinting explain their willingness to perform and to participate in the production process. Swans manifest a multiplicity of facts that are deployed in different ways to realise their different realities.

Finally, what a conversation between STS and screen studies generates is another approach to thinking about the constructed nature of wildlife TV. Beyond all the acknowledgement in media studies of television's manipulation of animals and the natural world, there is a lingering concern about representational adequacy and the effects of such manipulations. Often, media animals are critiqued as evidence of ideological or economic imperatives, as yet another demonstration of what humans *do* to animals. But this approach pays little attention to the actual logistics of making animals televisual, to the relations and interactions between animals, technical devices and humans. When some of those relations are revealed, as MODs partially enable, ideological intentionality is hard to pin down. Instead, we see complexity and the dynamics of emergence; how a reality is provoked and crafted rather than found and represented. Disclosing the logistics through which imprinted birds, 3D cameras and their people gather, "The Making of David Attenborough's the Conquest of the Skies" (Colossus Productions, 2014) provides significant insights into the dynamics of composing multiple whooper swan televisual realities. The question is not how faithful such realities are to animal lives lived beyond mediation. Rather, we must ask: How are these realities provoked and how do they extend or inhibit the capacity of television to be a multispecies contact zone inviting human attunement to animals and their diverse modes of being?

Part Three: Inhabiting

A central focus of natural history film has been the animal in its milieu. The genre's raison d'être has been the visual presentations of how animals inhabit worlds. Inhabitation, however, is not the preserve of the animal subjects alone. In this part we explore how natural history content also enrols viewers in distinct processes of inhabiting. In the examples we examine in the following two chapters we consider how the programs analysed situate viewers and convey a sense of dwelling, how they develop distinct points of view that configure viewers as inhabiting particular worlds. In this way, we are interested in the visual and narrative techniques through which different modes of occupation are provoked. By advancing the notion of inhabiting, we also seek to identify how the programs examined generate relations of being in common, of belonging, of responsibility and of care – how viewers are implicated, for example, in the natural world as a form of national patrimony or are invited to experience a sense of planetary interconnectedness.

By reviewing a number of landmark natural history films produced by the ABC since the late 1980s, we explore different permutations of this process of inhabitation. Through our examples, we draw a distinction – at once historical and political – between inhabitation as a process of inhabiting the national, on the one hand, and inhabiting the planetary, on the other. In making this contrast, we demonstrate how inhabiting a nation and situating televisual animals and environments in the time-space of the nation is a vastly different process from inhabiting the planetary, where a sense of the planet is provoked for television audiences, where humans and nonhuman animals are situated as planetary beings interconnected through earth-systems processes.

In Chapter 5 we examine national inhabitation as a distinct mode of dwelling: one that works through *nationing natural history*. The idea of "nationing" has been used by analysts to describe the processes of cultural consumption and production through which a national identity, heritage and culture is constructed.[1] We build on this notion to argue that nationing is not limited to practices of identity construction. Rather, in our account, the process of nationing involves a particular ethos of inhabitation. It is concerned with distinct ways of relating to others – human and nonhuman – that are primarily figured in relation to the temporal and spatial co-ordinates of the nation. In this way, it is an ethos of inhabitation, a modality of dwelling, that is inseparable from the ways the nation is inscribed into the history and geography of a place. It is, then, an inhabitation indissoluble from the narration of nation. The ABC series we explore in Chapter 5 exemplifies this process of dwelling, as national subjects come to be hailed as heirs to a unique natural patrimony. In Chapter 6 we examine programs that are inflected less by the ethos of national dwelling, and more by an overwhelming sense of the environmental crisis as a planetary predicament. This predicament or crisis is unconstrained by geopolitical borders of nation-states or by the cultural boundaries of national imaginaries, and it involves all living things. The examples in this chapter explore modes of inhabitation in which humans, animals and environments are implicated in the spatio-temporal scale of the planetary, and in which local events are inseparable from planetary processes, where local dwelling is simultaneously a planetary inhabitation.

The questions driving our analysis in this section, then, concern the ways in which televisual animals and screen environments are enrolled in the process of inhabitation and how they are implicated in different modes or senses of dwelling – modes that have profound consequences

---

[1]   Bennett 1995; Rowe, Turner and Waterton 2018; Turner 1993.

Part Three: Inhabiting

for the ways the lives of nonhuman others are made public and the relations of responsibility for such lives are established and negotiated for audiences.

5
The *Nature of Australia* series
Nationing nature

Early in 1981 an "Inter-office Memo" was circulated to staff at the ABC. The subject line read: "Bicentenary Year".[1] Seven years out from the bicentenary, senior management were busy soliciting ideas from their television department for possible contributions to mark the year in question: 1988. While acknowledging that "at this stage any idea is unlikely to be more than a twinkle in the eye", the memo signalled the upcoming national anniversary as a major event for the broadcaster. Content producers were asked for initiatives that would meet the ABC Charter[2] in relation to this national event. It is worth quoting at length a document written three years later by John Vandenbeld, the then Director of the Natural History Unit (NHU). This pitched the show that would later be developed as the ABC's major bicentennial contribution. Entitled "The nature of Australia: aims", this text gives a sense of how natural history television was envisioned as a central device linking

---

1 Humphrey Fisher (1981). Inter-office Memo: Bicentenary Year. 1 April 1981. ABC NHU Archive, Box 12/4751.
2 The ABC Charter is contained in s6 of the *Australian Broadcasting Corporation Act* 1983, where the functions and responsibilities of the ABC include: "broadcasting programs that contribute to a sense of national identity and inform and entertain, and reflect the cultural diversity of the Australian community; and ... broadcasting programs of an educational nature."

the ABC's public service imperatives – of informing, educating and entertaining Australians – with the occasion of the "Bicentenary Year".

Underscoring the significance of the nation's natural environment for this project, Vandenbeld wrote:

> Anniversaries are rather artificial occasions, recalling no more than an arbitrary point in time. Yet they do serve to direct attention to matters that normally remain overshadowed by more immediate day-to-day concerns. They provide useful moments for a community to pause and reflect on where it's come from and where it means to go. For Australians in the bicentenary year of the founding of their community, an inseparable element of such reflection must be the physical nature of their environment for it directly *determines* the nature of their community.[3]

Building on this assertion, that it is the physical environment that defines the character of the Australian community, Vandenbeld outlined his plan for a watershed natural history documentary. It would be a major cultural marker for the national population, providing an informative and emotive mediation of the natural world that has come to define them, but also how they might continue their relationship with it into the future. In a statement on how Australians might come to dwell on the continent and live with its natural environments, Vandenbeld offered a powerful framing of inhabiting as an expression of ecological nationalism. His central concern was how to have a "relationship with the land":

> The Nature of Australia will ... make a coherent television account of the natural history of the island continent to explain simply, clearly and entertainingly how Australia and the things that live on and around it came to be the way they are; to explore the complex relationships of climate, landscape, plants and animals – to find in what ways the Australian environment is different from those of the rest of the world, and in what ways it

---

3   John Vandenbeld (1984). The nature of Australia: aims. ABC NHU Archive, Box 12/4751. (Our emphasis).

5 The *Nature of Australia* series

is the same. It will endeavour to bring the Australian community, in the 200th year of its founding, a new awareness to inform – if it so wishes – its future relationship with the land.[4]

Vandenbeld went on to underscore the importance of key elements of the natural history genre – of telling, enthralling and informing – to realise this ambition: "To serve as an effective vehicle for these aims, the *Nature of Australia* series must succeed on a number of levels: on the simplest level, the varied and spectacular nature of the subject material will make it visually enthralling. The material will be organised to tell the story simply and well, conveying information together with a sense of wonder and delight."[5] In the context of the forthcoming bicentennial celebrations, Vandenbeld's pitch foregrounded the potential for natural history television to serve the national project and provoke a form of national dwelling. The series would explain to viewers where they lived and how this environment shaped them and how they need to relate to it into the future.

Four years in the making, *Nature of Australia: A Portrait of the Island Continent* (ABC, 1988), as it was formally titled, was to be the realisation of Vandenbeld's vision.[6] The show was produced in collaboration with the BBC, the US public broadcaster and the Australian Heritage Commission, the federal body charged with responsibility for bicentennial events.[7] Rumoured to have cost in excess of three million Australia dollars, the show was the most expensive

---

4   John Vandenbeld (1984). The nature of Australia: aims. ABC NHU Archive, Box 12/4751.
5   John Vandenbeld (1984). The nature of Australia: aims. ABC NHU Archive, Box 12/4751.
6   The six-part series first screened weekly on ABC TV between 15 May and 19 June 1988.
7   The series was screened on the BBC in 1988. John Spark, Director of the BBC's Natural History Unit, was to praise the series, writing to Vandenbeld: "It looks expensive, the films are glossy and the stories are coherent. The overall effect is one of quality and stature and they measure well against our own productions" (6 June 1988, ABC NHU Archive, Box 12/4751). The series' New York co-producers, WNET, remixed the programs, where they were broadcast in late 1988 as a mini-series in season seven of WNET's long-running series, *Nature*.

natural history series made in Australia and widely considered the summit of the ABC Natural History Unit's creative achievement. Produced by Vandenbeld and Dione Gilmour (who was to succeed Vandenbeld as the NHU's director), the visually spectacular six-part documentary series showcased the cinematic talents of the cameramen, David Parer AO and Neil Rettig. Robyn Williams, already well-known to Australian audiences as host of ABC radio's *Science Show*, narrated the series.[8] Kevin Hocking's lush score, performed by the Melbourne Symphony Orchestra, accompanied the footage.[9]

The series took a broadly geographical approach. Each episode focused on a distinct environment: the marine worlds of the Great Australian Bight and the Great Barrier Reef (Episode 2); "the bush" as characterised by the eucalypt forests of south-eastern Australia (Episode 3); the arid desert interior of Lake Eyre (Episode 4); and the cycles of drought and deluge of northern Australia (Episode 5). This penultimate episode also included a segment concentrating on "how the seasons determine the pattern of life for the Aboriginal people". However, these regionally-orientated episodes dedicated to particular environments were book-ended by shows that narrated the series within a broad temporal arch. The first episode, entitled – with an ironic nod to Charles Darwin – "A Separate Creation", explored the continent's Gondwanan connections, demonstrating its fauna and flora's evolutionary entanglements in deep time, and focused particularly on the triumph of the marsupials. The final episode, "The End of Isolation", was much more temporally truncated, and concentrated on the environmental impact of "the European invasion"

---

8   George Negus contended at the time that the series was "painlessly narrated – almost understated – by the scientific everyman of the ABC Robin [sic] Williams" (*Sydney Morning Herald*, 22 January 1989). Nevertheless, it is worth noting that in a global natural history film market, Williams' accent was viewed as problematic. While "fresh", his "hybrid inflexions" raised the consternation of the BBC co-producers; naturally, they pressed for Attenborough to do the voice-over. As far as UK audience reception was concerned, their anxiety proved unfounded (ABC NHU Archive, Box 12/4751). The US co-producers, WNET, did re-narrate the series with *Nature*'s host, George Page.

9   Hocking's score won the French Television Award for Best Documentary Score of that year.

5 The Nature of Australia series

of the past 200 years, and, in doing so, as the series blurb put it, "[told] the story of that invasion, which sent change sweeping across the continent with unprecedented speed". It was a series that delighted both audiences and critics, establishing *Nature of Australia* as the ABC's most significant contribution to the bicentenary.

Audience responses to the series' early screenings suggest the overall effect was arresting. Robin Hill recounted "many ooohs! and aaahs!" among the gush of enthusiasm "from a mixed audience" when he reported on an advance screening at the Melbourne Zoo.[10] Other media commentators also recorded captivated audiences, remarking on the sheer volume of "mind-boggling and jaw dropping" moments in the footage.[11] The show went on to enjoy broad critical acclaim and achieve huge audiences. It won numerous national and international awards, including: the Panda Awards (the "Green Oscars") at the prestigious Wildscreen Festival, Bristol, England; a Logie for Outstanding Single Documentary or Documentary Series; and an Australian Bicentennial Heritage Award. *Nature of Australia* was also a commercial and popular success.[12] Far exceeding the NHU's "wildest expectations", the series attained unprecedented audiences for a natural history documentary in Australia.[13] When *Nature of Australia* was screened in the United Kingdom on BBC Two, it also scored very high audience ratings, second only in popularity to snooker on that channel.[14] *Nature of Australia* also achieved significant sales in other international markets. Within the first year of its release, it had been sold to broadcasters in more than 20 countries. In addition, in the period immediately after the show's first broadcast, there were strong sales for various tie-ins in the domestic market. The series' video collection sold 110,000 VHS cassettes. And the companion book with the same title, authored by Vandenbeld, sold 50,000 copies within the first months of its publication. It was claimed that this commercial success saw the series "make its money back many times over in the ensuing years". According

---

10   Hill 1988, 63.
11   Gleitzman 1988.
12   Australian Broadcasting Commission, *Annual Report*, 1988.
13   ABC NHU Archive, Box 12/4751.
14   ABC NHU Archive, Box 12/4751.

to the series entry on the Australian Screen website, over 19 programs emerged from the series offcuts.[15]

Nature of Australia was no doubt a complex cultural product. While carefully crafted to meet the cultural nationalism demanded of the bicentenary, it was also designed to appeal to international markets by realising the global "blue chip" style of quality natural history productions. Championed by the BBC's Natural History Unit and synonymous with David Attenborough, the protocols of blue chip, as Derek Bousé has characterised them, demonstrate a commitment to presenting an aestheticised, "timeless" nature, beyond the human, untouched by history or politics or controversy.[16] To achieve a nationally significant and globally marketable blue chip series, *Nature of Australia*'s makers were in a tricky position. They had to perform a distinctly national nature, around which a national sentiment and ethos of dwelling could cohere, but this nature also needed to play for global audiences as a marker of an exotic wildlife, untouched and uncontaminated, which could compete with the global brand of Attenborough and BBC's Natural History Unit.[17] In this context, *Nature of Australia*'s televisual animals had to walk a difficult line: simultaneously, they had to present as animals that were natural, seemingly outside culture and uncontaminated by the modern, and that were national, somehow already contained by the nation and its cultural imaginary. That is: the animals presented had to be unquestionably natural *and* somehow already always Australian.

In many ways, the ABC's engagement with the bicentenary and its investment in *Nature of Australia* exemplified the process of "nationing". This term emerged in the field of Australian cultural studies as it developed in the 1980s and 1990s and was advanced as a concept to explore the ways in which the new discourses of cultural nationalism and their institutions and texts were articulated in relation to the formation of national subjects.[18] The strength of the concept was that it allowed analysts to review a range of purposes to which

---

15 https://aso.gov.au/titles/series/nature-of-australia/.
16 Bousé 2000, 14–15.
17 See Gouyon 2019; Richards 2013.
18 Turner 1993.

the production and representation of the nation was put, and also consider the ways in which the building of national cultural identity was folded into the country's cultural production and consumption. The bicentenary was an important moment for the development of this concept and scholarship. Here, attention was given to the process of "nationing history" through which national subjects were situated in specific spatio-temporal relations co-ordinated by the national imaginary. Central to this process was the role of various media and heritage practices. These constructed particular "past-present alignments" that were pressed into the service of a distinctive expression of Australian nationhood – specifically, a national past that aligned with the sensibilities of a "post-colonial" settler-state.[19] There has been a recent renewal of interest in nationing in relation to contemporary Australian culture.[20] We build on this literature by suggesting that nationing is not only a practice of identity building, it is also a process of inhabiting: a process of national dwelling. This process of nationing involves a particular ethics of inhabitation: an ethics or civics of relating to, of dwelling with others, human and nonhuman animals and environments, in the time-space of the nation. In this chapter we argue that *Nature of Australia* provokes a distinct mode of national inhabitation: one that works through a process of *nationing natural history*.

Nationing natural history

In an interview with British film-maker, Barry Paine, *Nature of Australia*'s (ABC, 1988) director and co-producer, Dione Gilmour, reflected on the show's success.[21] She echoed Ken Taylor's rationale for the ABC's commitment to nature documentary, which he had expressed on the eve of the ABC's NHU inauguration nearly two decades previously (see Chapter 2). In so doing, Gilmour implicitly underlined the continuity in the unit's raison d'être across the

---

19 Bennett 1995.
20 See Rowe, Turner and Waterton 2018.
21 Paine 2002.

intervening years: namely, that of delivering on the promise of bringing as yet unseen native animals to the nation's television screens. For Gilmour, the enduring importance of the *Nature of Australia* series rested on the ways it brought the nation's rich natural history to vision in new ways by bringing to public attention natural processes and animal behaviours that were little understood or appreciated by that audience. Gilmour contended: "A lot of those programmes showed Australians an Australia they didn't even know existed ... exposing Australians to what was there and showing them some reasons why things were there."[22] However, as Vandenbeld's pitch attests, there was much more going on in the series than the seemingly innocent revelation of unseen nature that Gilmour claims. The series' showing and telling was tightly co-ordinated within a national time-space that established links between contemporary Australians, the continent's natural environment and deep geological history. In this way, it framed natural history in terms of how distinct nature/environments shaped culture and determined particular modes of inhabiting. This built on a national imaginary that assumed temporal and spatial continuities which are belied by geological time and which are disrupted by Indigenous agency.

Our primary focus in examining *Nature of Australia* (ABC, 1988) is the cultural technologies and techniques by which this technically difficult and culturally significant "revelation" of Australian natural history was performed. We want to understand the distinct ways in which *Nature of Australia* made visual to its audiences the geological and biological processes shaping the continent and the species that live on it. In particular, we want to discover the ways in which this making public of the continent's long natural history – of showing "Australians an Australia they didn't even know existed" – performed a social reality that posited a geology and a biota in terms that were simultaneously *natural* and *national*.

In this way, not only did *Nature of Australia* come to frame the continent's wildlife as national, in performing the reveal of what Parer termed "our Australian cryptic ... elusive animals".[23] It also articulated

---

22 Paine 2002.
23 ABC NHU Archive, Box 12/4751.

an anachronistic conceit. This was performed through visual and narrative techniques that worked to weave national time (less than 200 years) into the fabric of the continent's deep time. In examining these techniques, we are interested in how geological events and zoological species were nationalised, were made Australian long before the nation was politically constituted. The question is: How did these geological narratives and natural history performances enrol Australian audiences as heirs to and inhabitants of a national nature? To pursue this question, we focus on two interconnected procedures through which this inhabitation was made possible: first, by making national nature a compelling televisual reality; and, second, by showing how inhabiting *Australian nature* involved complex and contradictory processes of possession and occupation, belonging and care.

Commenting on the triumph of the series on its first national screening, one television critic pronounced that "the star of *Nature of Australia* [was] Australia itself".[24] For a show that celebrated the continent's landscapes, ecologies and species, this declaration might well seem unremarkable and self-evident. Nevertheless, it begs the question: How did a series devoted to narrating geological and evolutionary processes that anchored the continent and its biota in deep time make a star out of the relatively recent geopolitical and cultural category, "Australia"? A category that, after all, has a very short history in relation to the 180 million years on which the Gondwanaland narrative rests and against which the series as a whole was staged. This territorial and cultural category, which has very little bearing on the expanse of geological and evolutionary time with which the series was ostensibly concerned, came to frame the content of the show in which everything that was shown was designated self-evidently "Australian".

Narratively, this nationing of nature gave the series its continuity and cohesion. It provided a frame on which to hang otherwise disjunctive temporalities, diverse ecologies and divergent species. However, if you are to believe the commentaries of the day, the allure of this national frame saw it emerge as the show's star. Audiences, it seems, were captivated by the framing device itself – Australia – and, somehow, were drawn into its orbit as it radiated a pulsating national

---

24 Wright 1988.

sign across the episodes and out across the continent's zoology and geology through various narrative, visual and sound techniques. How, then, did this nationing of natural history proceed?

One of the central strategies by which *Nature of Australia* performed this accomplishment was by subsuming deep time to "the time of the nation" itself and, in so doing, making a national natural history not just plausible to audiences but self-evident.[25] The series can be understood as an exercise in the nationalisation of deep time. Through this remarkable temporal feat, national subjects were hailed in a narration of geological and evolutionary time in which they were positioned as the natural inheritors to a national patrimony: an Australian nature. However, this was not simply a concern with the interpellation of a national subject captivated by the national sign/star, but rather with how the series performed a particular making public of deep time in which its contingent geological and biological processes were framed as always *already* national.

One of the key techniques by which deep time came to be overwritten by the national was through a process that Benedict Anderson has described as the "logoization of space".[26] This is clearly demonstrated, for example, in the opening episode of *Nature of Australia*. In this episode there is a visualisation of the process of the breaking up of Gondwanaland into the aggregate of southern landmasses whose shapes we now recognise as constitutive of the Southern Hemisphere as it appears on contemporary maps of the world. This sequence presented in mere seconds a process that had been accomplished over hundreds of millions of years. For Australian viewers, this visualisation performed a certain geological-cum-cartographic birth of the nation as the familiar outline of the island continent morphed into shape and drifted into its present global location. Similarly, in the same episode, this cartography served to nationalise prehistoric creatures. Animals from the Cenozoic period were framed as "Australian" on the premise that they once existed on a landmass that is now geopolitically designated under the national rubric and made visual in cartographic form recognised territorially as Australia. This was only made possible by the matching of physical

---

25   Bhabha 1994.
26   Anderson 1991, 163–85.

5 The *Nature of Australia* series

geographical boundaries with political borders. Realising the mantra of Australia's first prime minister, Edmund Barton, "a nation for a continent and a continent for a nation", it was a confluence secured in 1901 with the federation of the Australian colonies. In the opening episode of *Nature of Australia*, then, the map of the geological emergence of the continent was used to solicit a cartographic performance in which the events of deep time appeared to have happened already in national space long, long before the nation existed. With this sleight of hand, these prehistoric creatures and their heirs came to be enrolled in a national project: making nature Australian.

If the "exploration on screen of time passing" is always, as Therese Davis and Belinda Smaill contend, "a situated and ideological endeavour",[27] the devices nationalising deep time in *Nature of Australia* need to be situated in relation to a crisis in "the narration of nation" represented by the date, 26 January 1788. This is the day when, in a demonstration of imperial sovereignty, the Union Jack first fluttered at Sydney Cove above Arthur Phillip (later to become the first governor of the colony of New South Wales) and his grim entourage. This is a date that is as controversial as it is foundational for Australian nationhood, marking the advent of the continent's European invasion. It is a date that stands as a turning point in the continent's natural and cultural history, one that designates the beginning of an ambivalent historical achievement: Australian modernity. This was a mixed accomplishment that the bicentennial event brought to public attention. For a critical moment in 1988, the contestations of the historical legacy of the European appropriation of the land, and the dispossession of the Indigenous peoples who dwelt in it, were at the heart of public debate. The bicentennial event was central to critical developments in the country's cultural institutions and cultural policy and with it a new national discourse that sought to contend with the state's colonial legacy, with mixed results.[28]

Nevertheless, seemingly in the belief that natural history was without a political history, the approach of the *Nature of Australia* series was to tactically avoid the controversy of bicentennial celebrations

---

27   Davis and Smaill 2018, 33.
28   See Bennett, Buckridge et al. 2000.

altogether by largely sidestepping the 200 years in contention. This strategy carefully circumvented questions of Indigenous dispossession. One pundit, in reviewing the cultural events of the bicentennial year, located the series' success in precisely this strategy of avoidance: "*Nature of Australia* was so popular on the ABC, because it was so safe."[29] In this context, *Nature of Australia*'s presentations of the natural world provided a diversion and respite from some of the unsettling cultural politics of settler colonialism that the bicentenary brought to the fore.

However, while this avoidance many have been politically safe, it was hardly benign. By taking as its focus the deep time of the continent's formation and evolution, Indigenous peoples were left to arrive late in Episode 5. Human–animal–environment relations 65,000 years in the making were sparingly treated in *Nature of Australia*.[30] In a short closing segment in the penultimate episode, pre-European Indigenous populations were not romanticised as primitive, which would cast them in a continuity with nature. *Nature of Australia* was quick to distance itself from such familiar and disturbing colonial tropes. Rather than "being a timeless people in a timeless land", Indigenous populations were presented as active agents of radical environmental modification. Elaborating on the profound material and spiritual importance of fire to Indigenous culture, the sequence focused on how the Indigenous development and dispersal of fire techniques over many millennia of inhabitation significantly altered the continent's ecologies, dramatically transforming "the nature of Australia". In this way, Indigenous populations were presented as the first wave of the continent's human colonisation whose ecologically transformative pyro-culture foreshadowed, but was dramatically exceeded by, the environmental destruction of 200 years of an increasingly fossil-fuelled European settlement.

This sequence thus provided the bridge to the final episode, which was devoted to the continent's post-1788 environmental history. In

---

29 1988: The restless year. *Sydney Morning Herald* 5 December 1988, 69.
30 This is in marked contrast to Parer's earlier work with the NHU, particularly his work in PNG, which focused intensively on the relations of Indigenous peoples and their animals.

5 The *Nature of Australia* series

Eurocentric terms, and belying the deep Gondwana entanglements that the earlier episodes had explicated as well as ignoring long-established Indigenous trading networks extending north of the continent, the final episode was tellingly titled, "The End of Isolation".

In one sense, there is nothing Australian about the first five episodes of *Nature of Australia* in that they purport to present an exclusively nonhuman and largely pre-human world in which the geopolitical-cultural entity, Australia, could only ever be a bold anachronism. However, in the context of the bicentenary, the back-projection of a natural Australia opened a geopolitics of Gondwana – and those of subsequent geological intervals – in a curious act of disenfranchisement. By positing an Australian deep time that massively overshadowed the duration of an Indigenous presence on the continent, the show situated that presence in an already existing national nature and patrimony, hundreds of millions of years in the making. Despite organising the content of Episode 5, which focuses on the continent's tropical north, according to the designations of the Indigenous seasonal calendar, this is a disjunctive temporality that is quickly assumed by national time. Narratively, the continent's Indigenous peoples find themselves already in the national frame as first Australians, long before the first Europe colonialists arrive; theirs became histories dwarfed by the luminosity of the national star, as a geological and evolutionary event, that predated any human settlement by a vast sway of geological time.

Nature of Australia was an exercise in national narration that offered a variation on Anderson's observation on nationalist discourse. The nation, he insists, is a primordial construct – one that "always looms out of an immemorial past".[31] In the case of *Nature of Australia*, however, the primordial is not so much mythic but geologic. The postulation of an Australian deep time was also a move, it would seem, that could only fudge Indigenous priorities. Their legitimacy is one founded on a continuous Indigenous presence that existed long before the imposition of the settler-nation as both an imaginary and institutional set of arrangements on the continent. In this sense, then, an Australian deep time is not simply anachronistic. It is a form of

---

31   Anderson 1991, 51.

temporal colonisation. It asserts settler priorities in relation to the human and the nonhuman by assuming a nation container as one that has always been – forgetting temporalities that proceed autonomously from that container. In this way, *Nature of Australia*'s back-projection of a nationalised deep time continued a mode of colonial violence. The inhabitation of a national nature that this series solicited was a form of colonial dwelling. It perpetuated an ethos of dispossession.

If the "post-colonial" politics of the "bicentennial celebration" was one controversy in which *Nature of Australia* was enmeshed, another was the environment crisis: the unintended consequence accompanying the continent's modernisation that the bicentenary celebrated. Unlike the issue of Indigenous dispossession that surrounded the bicentennial events, and which the *Nature of Australia* strangely perpetuated by playing it "safe", the series' final episode directly addressed this second controversy. This episode in many ways was a striking departure from those that preceded it. The blue chip protocols and values that characterised the previous episodes and presented a specular, largely ahistorical and apolitical "nature" gave way to "the environment" and its need for conservation. With frequent use of historical footage, this shift was accompanied by a mode of presentation more familiar to social documentary. This is exemplified in a sequence on the Australian dust bowl. During the 1930s and 1940s, drought and soil erosion devastated the ecology and economy of rural hinterlands, while dust storms choked eastern seaboard cities. The voice-over to this sequence informs the audience that it was in this period that "an urgent new word joined the vocabulary of political debate – conservation". This was underscored with footage from an address by the Hon. William Scully, Minister of Commerce and Agriculture, in 1944. Scully solemnly stated:

> The land devastation and erosion is largely due to ignorance and exploitation. Our destruction of natural timbers and herbage, plus overstocking of the land is the primary cause of soil erosion by wind and water. If we do not turn from exploitation to conservation we shall without question destroy our national heritage.

This was a sentiment largely endorsed by the final episode. It offered multiple permutations on the environmental and ecological consequences of the European colonisation and modernisation of the Australian continent, but maintained that the heirs to this legacy had the capacity for repair. Here the human, largely in its European settler-colonial form, was cast as an ambivalent figure, as both exploiter and protector of the natural world. This subject was presented as one cleaved between two positions: one in which nature was a resource for modernisation to exploit; and another in which nature was a national patrimony to be curated – to be conserved and protected, cared for.

However, in this episode, where the spectre of climate change was acknowledged in an early public statement on the morphing of the human into the geological, the organising division between Australians and their natural world was showing signs of unravelling.[32] This might well be the full import of the final episode's title, the "End of Isolation". The early episodes and the stories of the continent's "Gondwana Connection" are not ones of isolation but indeed of connections, of geological and evolutionary links that connect the animals and plants that are dispersed across a now dis-contiguous southern landmass. The "End of Isolation", however, concerns not the tectonic forces dividing Gondwana but the shock of the first phase of globalisation on the continent's life.

However, it was not just about the advent of modernity on the island continent, it was also a recognition of the entanglements of the human and the nonhuman, which belie the division between nature and culture through which wildlife and its environment that populate the series was performed. This delivers the series' great irony: the geological past that the series worked hard to nationalise had, in the final episode, morphed into a geological future to which the nation's fate was tied. The imaginary back-projection of the nation into a deep geological past of the earlier episodes was displaced in the final episode

---

32 There is no doubt that 1988 was a big year for Australian cultural politics, but it was also a significant year in the politics of climate change. This was the year that NASA scientist, James Hansen, famously addressed the US Congress on the imminent risks from global heating and formally put climate change on the political table, where it was to languish.

by a new geological present-becoming-future – the forward-projection of an Australian modernity now folding into a geological reality: the climate crisis.

This emerging geological condition was presented not only as the driver of a national future to be averted, but also as an unprecedented planetary predicament. The nation in this episode no longer colonises geological time in the fabrication of a national deep time. Rather, Australian modernity is now folded into geological time itself as an entity contributing to an alternation in the earth's biogeochemical systems, which the nation now faces as its climate future. This change in orientation is perhaps foreshadowed in the opening scene of the final episode: no longer sweeping panoramas of sublime natural landscapes bathed in sunlight, the vision turns noir with night footage of the Sydney Harbour precinct. We see the Bridge and Opera House, no doubt the structures most iconic of an Australian modernity and ones most overexposed in the bicentennial celebrations. But this footage is in contrast to sunny touristic representations: it is at night, street level, edgy. It seems to suggest vulnerability, foreboding: an unsettling of any easy inhabitation of a national nature. And it is precisely this unsettlement of the Australian settlement that threads through the final episode. Australian modernity is demonstrated again and again to be a precarious achievement, conditional on enormous environmental degradation and loss and numerous species extinctions. A rift is finally seeded between the nation and nature, whose obfuscation in the mists of geological time made it possible in the earlier episodes to dwell in the conceit of a national nature. But perhaps the unhomely presentation of the Harbour precinct also foreshadows an emerging dis-ease with a new planetary nature. It is now difficult to see the precinct's steel and concrete structures and not recall their emerging geohistory, be it the trails of carbon emissions of international air travel in which they are enmeshed as talisman of global tourism, or the long afterlife of the material composites of which they are composed, now destined to settle into the strata as testimony to the human species' geological agency.[33]

In the style of the final episode there is, then, the beginning of a shift in the register of inhabiting. The environmental crisis cannot be

---

33   Dibley 2018.

5 The *Nature of Australia* series

contained by the nation and its narration. It cannot be convincingly confined to the process of nationing natural history that the preceding episodes exemplify. There is, then, a profound fading of the national star. Rather, life on the continent is not delimited by a national geology and nationalist ecology, but returned to the earthly processes to which it is bound – this time not with those of Gondwana, but those we would have to wait a decade or so to name as the Anthropocene.[34]

In the final episode, these anthropocenic entanglements are most tellingly articulated in a sequence on environmental management in the Tanami Desert in northern Australia. In many ways, this sequence serves as a bicentennial redemption or post-colonial rapprochement in which, as stated in the episode, the combining of "modern science and traditional practices offers hope". This concerns the presentation of new approaches to the management of the environment exemplified in contemporary fire and land management practices that have sought to harmonise Indigenous knowledge with scientific techniques. The sequence presents approaches that look to mitigate fire risk and restore desert ecosystems by blending the traditional knowledge of Indigenous fire practices, cultural burning, with satellite and digital imaging for the analysis and management of fire-prone environments. The vision shifts between smoke drifts and crackling desert spinifex and pixelated satellite images of expanding and retreating hotspots. This is followed by close-ups of small marsupials, including rare bilbys, whose future, viewers are informed, might be assured with this innovative approach. Strangely, while footage of scientists tapping on keyboards in their laboratory captures the labour of "remote sensing", the practitioners of cultural burning and their work in managing local ecologies make no appearance on screen.

While *Nature of Australia* was in many ways an exquisite performance in the nationing of natural history, it also demonstrated the limits of this strategy. Nationing natural history and the process of national inhabitation it sought to solicit could only occur in a disjunctive time. The imperatives of geological time, biological time, Indigenous time and the time of global modernity, ultimately, as the series' final episode confirmed, could not be subordinated to the

---

34   Crutzen 2002.

national sign. Inconsistent, incomparable, unconnected temporalities ruptured the national container, and with it other modes of inhabitation beyond the national increasingly registered their significance for the series: foremost among them were the Indigenous and the planetary.

Tellingly, the final episode, where the imbroglios post-1788 were acknowledged, was excised for certain international markets. This was possibly done to preserve the blue chip status of the earlier episodes and eliminate any sense of politics from the series. The DVD set sold by the ABC did not include it, maintaining the series' presentation of a natural world that was outside controversy and outside modern time.[35] Australian nature, it was deemed, was no longer interesting for international markets once it became historical and political; that is, compromised by the modern and its mess of contaminations and contestations. The national sign could signal the exotic, but not the modern, and certainly not a shared planetary predicament. Nor could it accommodate a mode of inhabitation that recognised this precarious interconnectedness of being planetary.

---

35 A version of the final episode was screened on WHYY PBS (Philadelphia and Delaware, USA) on 18 December 1988, although the material on climate change was omitted.

6
After nature, after animals
Inhabiting a damaged planet

The Natural History Unit (NHU) was closed in 2007. Director of Television at the ABC at the time, Kim Dalton, justified this decision on two grounds. First, the programs were hugely expensive to produce, especially when they had to meet the standards of overseas buyers or co-creators, and second, natural history content, he argued, would still be produced by the documentaries division of the ABC.[1] In reality, the move was part of a wider shift in the ABC towards outsourcing or commissioned content. For Dalton, outsourcing opened up the possibility of generating a wider diversity of natural history programs and stimulating the local independent production sector. For others, the decision represented the inexorable decline of the ABC as an in-house production house and its conversion into a "transmitter for hire".[2]

The closure of the NHU generated protest from a number of different groups. Prominent scientists, members of the Wilderness Society, Friends of the ABC and President of the Australian Conservation Foundation were all signatories to a letter to the ABC Board accusing the organisation of abandoning its charter and failing to keep the community informed about "what we have and what we

---

1   Dyer 2007.
2   Leung 2007.

are at risk of losing".[3] This letter pointed out the ethical obligations of the ABC both to its audiences *and* to nature. While members of the independent production sector were initially excited at the prospect of more funds being made available for commissioned work, the closure did not deliver the funds and commissions that were anticipated. There was a real decline in natural history content.

Over the years since the closure, the ABC has maintained a commitment to commissioning or screening natural history and factual environmental content from a wide variety of sources. Whether the amount of this content matches the heady days of the 1980s and 1990s is not the issue. Our concern is with how the shift to outsourcing has generated different approaches to screening nature and animals and different political effects. This brings us to a series of programs screened in December 2020 released under the badge of Your Planet. In various on-air and online promotions, the focus of the series was described as "the changing environment and solutions to climate change".[4] Programs screened included *Big Weather: And How to Survive It* (Northern Pictures, 2020), *Wild Australia: After the Fires* (Northern Pictures, 2020), *Reef Live* (Northern Pictures, 2020) and *David Attenborough: Extinction* (BBC, 2020). These programs sometimes made for very uncomfortable viewing. Their credibility as entertaining factual or natural history content was challenged by disturbing imagery and bleak accounts of the impacts of climate change on humans, environments and animals.

Throughout the long evolution of natural history television on the ABC, there has been an implicit contract with audiences that "nature" will always be there, that it didn't just have a history but also a future. The Your Planet season broke that contract. The persistence of regeneration and natural resilience was called into question with scenes of catastrophic landscape destruction, wild weather and much more. Of course, this bleak content didn't completely dominate; it was balanced by appeals to hope – "we still have time" – as well as explorations of various scientific and technological solutions to looming planetary disaster. There was also footage of some spectacular natural events.

---

3   Leung 2007.
4   https://www.abc.net.au/your-planet/.

Reef Live, for example, was built on the promise of showing actual footage of coral spawning on prime-time television. However, even with these optimistic elements, the overwhelming affect was of loss and uncertainty. Nature no longer seemed to be a stable referent.

The Your Planet series signalled a significant shift in natural history programming on the ABC. While climate change and serious environmental damage had been explored before, these issues were generally marginal to the primary focus on engaging explorations of the natural world. In this series, these confronting issues were the main content and this displaced some long-established natural history codes. Ecological collapse, extinction and catastrophic natural destruction all indicated that the environment was becoming highly unstable largely due to human activities – the Anthropocene had arrived on television. How then to assess this shift? Do these programs constitute a new subgenre that could perhaps be called *post* natural history? Or are they an inevitable acknowledgement of worlds coming undone and the impossibility of sustaining previous narratives? For some reviewers, programs like those screened in the Your Planet season were evidence of the belated arrival of "socially responsible nature programming".[5] The messages in these programs might be difficult for audiences to hear, but environmental awareness can no longer be built on denial. If natural history documentaries are predicated on a fundamental commitment to factual information, then it was time to face *all* the facts.

While the pragmatism of this assessment is reasonable, it implicitly valorises facts and information as the most socially responsible approach to representing drastic environmental decline. This can obscure the affective and ethical registers of these programs, particularly the ways in which they wrestle with difficult questions about how to understand, let alone represent, the world's displacements; how to witness catastrophic loss in the age of the Anthropocene. These difficult questions generated a troubling subtext in the Your Planet season. While they may not have been explicitly stated, they haunted many of the visual sequences and narration. Each program approached them in different ways. Cumulatively, they added

---

5   Mangan 2019.

up to a profound reconfiguration of what counts as natural history television in an era when the continuing livability of the earth is in question.

Our focus in this final part is "inhabiting". In the previous chapter, "Australia" was configured as an extraordinary natural environment that exceeded the temporal and spatial boundaries of national geopolitics. *Nature of Australia* (ABC, 1988) nationalised nature and invited audiences to identify with an environment that they both inhabited and inherited as national subjects. In this chapter, we want to explore "inhabiting" in ways that transcend the idea of habitats or environments as fixed spaces. Our focus is on the processes whereby living things occupy the world and the ways in which these processes are configured and mediated by various socio-ecological systems – large and small. In the Your Planet season, the planet was occasionally mentioned as a locational reference point. However, what was far more powerful and significant was the creation of what Ursula Heise has described as a "sense of planet";[6] that is, a deterritorialisation of the links between culture, place and environment and a recognition of how humans, animals and habitats are mutually implicated in whole-earth processes. Even though the reef spawning and the 2019–20 Black Summer bushfires were framed as distinctively Australian events, they were also recognised as planetary, as part of a world in which ecologies are more than local and subject to forces far beyond the scope of national conservation or environmental management programs. The diverse forms of life captured in these programs inhabited a world shaped by irruptions and novelty that challenged notions of self-stabilising ecologies and natural resilience. Coral bleaching on the reef, extreme storms, wildfires and mass extinction events gave audiences a "sense of planet" where *all* modes of life were under serious threat.

Using programs from the ABC's 2020 Your Planet season, our aim is to understand what it means to contextualise nature and wildlife in a planetary framework. Does this spell the end of natural history programming as we know it or demand a necessary recalibration with the potential to amplify the public and political impact of the genre?

---

6   Heise 2008.

6 After nature, after animals

Can the codes and conventions of natural history programming imagine the socio-ecological present, let alone future, when environments are in a state of collapse? Several key themes will be examined. The first relates to Heise's idea of sense of planet: How is this sense framed in mass broadcast screen cultures and what kinds of ecological agency are planetary processes accorded? The second concerns the ways in which these programs enable distinct kinds of affective and ethical witnessing. If we are living in an age of loss, how does natural history television mediate this? Then there are the issues of time and scale. In *Reef Live*, for example, audiences were given access to a remarkable natural event screened live from remote underwater locations. This was promoted as "landmark natural history television" without recourse to computer-generated imagery (CGI) or other gimmicks, the underwater footage generating an experience of "becoming with" a massive and vital reproductive event. But the immediacy of this natural event was shadowed by a range of other pre-recorded expository content that focused on the extent of the losses caused by a series of recent coral bleachings; Indigenous connections to the reef over thousands of years; and research by scientists exploring how corals could adapt to warmer oceans in the future. While celebrations of the power of liveness and direct witness drove this program, this temporal effect was continually displaced by references to past natural abundance and the possibility of future disappearance. The diverse socio-ecological temporalities and scales in *Reef Live* made trouble for the excitement about biological vitalism or the idea of seeing nature perform – here and now! Finally, there is the question of science and its role in authorising what counts as planetary natural history on television. How was scientific knowledge and the figure of the field scientist enrolled in these programs? How did scientific modes of observing and inhabiting devastated landscapes provoke scientists and other experts to display a planetary perspective characterised by grief, not just facts and data?

Megafires and sense of planet

After the Fires (Northern Pictures, 2020) was promoted using the familiar natural history brand that the ABC has deployed for more than 50 years: Wild Australia; as well as being part of the Your Planet series.[7] However, with this program the exhaustion of the brand was revealed. As the press kit explained: "The fires of Australia's Black Summer are now recognised as the worst wildlife disaster in modern history", signalling that their scale and significance extended far beyond a local or national natural disaster. The promo continued: "The film provides an urgent message to safeguard our environment and bring about the necessary intervention required to maintain biodiversity on our hotter, more fiery planet, before it is too late" (Northern Pictures Press Kit, 2020). This sense of urgency implied that it was difficult to celebrate the enduring presence of *wild* Australia when three billion wildlife were estimated to be lost, many populations never to recover, and an area roughly the size of the UK burned. Nor could action or intervention be confined to Australia when a "more fiery planet" was now the reality. While brand recognition was the obvious motivation for promoting *After the Fires* as part of the ABC's longstanding Wild Australia tradition, this created an uneasy tension. Well-worn natural history visual codes, from spectacular animals to majestic remote landscapes, were disrupted with images of charred carcasses and drone shots of silent, blackened forests as far as the eye could see.

The program begins with a familiar natural history framing: fire has shaped the nature of Australia for millennia and has contributed to its international reputation as a "land of extremes". The tone then shifts dramatically as the voice-over tells the viewer that 2019 was the hottest and driest year on record and the Black Summer fires, which had begun earlier than ever before, were not only the most savage on record, they also "brought many species to the brink". Accompanying

---

7 "Wild Australia" was the term used to brand natural history programs before the establishment of the Natural History Unit in 1973. The first Wild Australia series was screened in 1971 and focused on the Antarctic. This framing of natural history or variations on it like Wildscreen (1991–96) or Wild Australasia (2003–04) persisted for many decades.

this bleak opening narration by Australian actor Hugo Weaving is a horrifying image of a group of kangaroos desperately fleeing a huge wall of fire racing towards them across a paddock. Animal terror writ large. Weaving then explains that animals that had been well adapted to fire events were facing a looming extinction crisis: "their world was now on fire ... whole animal cultures have been lost". The rest of the program visits a range of different locations that had experienced devastating fires and huge loss of animal life, including Kangaroo Island in South Australia where 40,000 koalas were estimated to have been killed. Those that remained had lost eighty per cent of their habitat. Footage of shrivelled koala carcasses lying in blackened landscapes are intercut with a local couple searching for surviving animals, assessing their wounds and taking them back to an army-run rescue shelter staffed by vets and volunteers: bare life in emergency times.

The Black Summer fires in Australia attracted global news coverage, much of it devoted to the human impacts and the sheer scale and elemental force of the fire front. What made *After the Fires* distinctive was its commitment to documenting the impacts on wildlife, to telling animal stories. The vast destruction of habitats and forests had created unrecognisable places stripped of life, offering no food, shelter or water to animal survivors. As one scientist remarks to camera as he walks through the desolation, "there's no life, not a single bird sound, animals reduced to ash – a shocking sight". Despite the express aim of the program to chart "ecological recovery", to affirm the idea of natural resilience, this objective was hard to realise. The evidence exceeded this. It also made it difficult to explain and contain the fires in an Australian context, to represent them as just another natural calamity in the onward march of national progress. Australia may have been the location of the fires, its environmental history a contributing factor, but the characteristics of these fires indicated bigger forces at work and a bigger reality beyond the national. The fires were a rupture, an event after which things would not be the same. Equally significant was the way in which the program acknowledged animals as being at the frontline of the global climate and biodiversity crisis. The size of the losses of biodiversity were noted as dramatically accelerating mass extinctions that were in train before the fires. Human actions, from land clearing to fossil fuels to intense urbanisation, were contributing to major changes in earth systems and the rise of a proposed geological epoch characterised by humans' use of fire called the Pyrocene. All these uncomfortable facts entered the narrative, and their effect was to implicitly recognise planetary processes and what was happening to them as a critical context.

References to the planet and planetary forces have an important history in wildlife programs. The rise of this framing is largely attributed to David Attenborough and his powerful determining influence on the genre.[8] As Morgan Richards argues, Attenborough effectively globalised BBC wildlife programming conceptually and economically when he turned his landmark series, *Life on Earth* (BBC, 1979), into an international marketing success story.[9] The series was made for a national audience and attracted huge ratings. However, it was also sold to over a hundred territories and was eventually watched by millions around the world. It turned BBC natural history content into a global brand. However, it wasn't just any natural history content. According to Richards, what made *Life on Earth* globally successful was its development of an entirely new framework for representing wild animals. This landmark television series didn't focus on particular ecologies or species, it explored "complex and diverse scientific ideas using footage and narratives from around the globe".[10] *Life on Earth* offered spectacular visions of diverse natural environments in order to explain the principles of evolutionary biology. Iconic images of the blue planet were central to promoting the idea of earth as a whole or unified system, as were sequences featuring Attenborough as a "televisual Darwin" roaming the world in order to explain the origins and evolution of life.[11]

The planetary, however, is not the same as the global. While Richards' focus is primarily on how BBC natural history content was commercialised and turned into a global brand, she also shows how this process could not have occurred without the development of a planetary vision of wildlife and ecologies that wrenched natural history

---

8   Gouyon 2019.
9   Richards 2013.
10   Richards 2013, 148.
11   Gouyon 2019, 224.

out of parochial local and national frameworks. With *Life on Earth*, Attenborough emerged as a closet Gaia thinker. While he didn't go in for the New Ageism that surrounded this term, he did explain and visualise key ideas from the earth sciences about a "living earth" and ecological interconnectedness. Subsequent series after *Life on Earth* gradually subsumed references to the earth or the "world around us" and became more explicitly focused on the planet. Shows like *Blue Planet* (BBC, 2001), *Planet Earth* (BBC, 2006) and *Our Planet* (Netflix, 2019) have been huge global commercial successes. They have also significantly developed the planetary framework using a distinct set of visual codes and cultural framings. Planet shows are promoted as landmark or blockbuster television outside the flow of regular natural history programming and promising far more. Since the turn of this century, they have steadily grown in budget and audience reach and now represent the high end of blue chip content: hugely expensive to produce, involving lots of spectacular footage, working across multiple platforms and driven by the logics of highly technologised modes of immersive spectatorship and awe.[12] The planet offers a framework for wildlife television where explanations of the fundamental order of things are promised.[13] However, it is not just a matter of understanding the whole but also the promise of seeing it.

There is no question that Attenborough and his planetary programs have played a critical role in representing the planet in distinct ways and in shaping audiences' understanding of ecological processes as interconnected and self-organising. Smaill considers his celebrity and reach as central to shaping a global environmental imagination in audiences, and that is a significant achievement.[14] However, what is less examined is how a planetary framing is actually configured and how different discourses about the planet and its agency affect the political impact of natural history programs. Attenborough's "sense of planet" might be hugely influential and dominant, but there are many other, less spectacular, ways of realising a planetary perspective and *After the Fires* was an important manifestation of this.

---

12 Louson 2018; Richards 2013.
13 Gouyon 2019, 224.
14 Smaill 2020.

Stories about animals – their experiences of the fire, their survival afterwards and the fate of their habitats – structured the program. This narrative strategy was obviously designed to generate empathy and concern in audiences, to orient them to the fate of animals and invite compassion. Many of the segments featured scientists, wildlife carers or local residents rescuing animal survivors, providing emergency food supplies or treating injuries. They also featured bleak assessments of whether *any* animal life was left in particular sites. However, despite this explicit commitment to documenting the animal experience of megafires, much of the program implicitly privileged human experience. The familiar humanist repertoire of natural history narrative techniques dominated: the ubiquitous voice-over framing the vision and how it should be apprehended; experts walking through landscapes and observing from a human scale. The overall effect was to position humans as separate from or outside the world represented – they may have been observing and mourning it, but ultimately they were reporting back from "the field". Mass animal death provoked sadness and sympathy for animals but also an anticipatory human grief about the future of humans. If animal life enriches, let alone supports, human life, if human interest in animals as scientific objects, as companion species, as radically other, underpins human ontological security, what happens to humans when animals disappear?

This anthropocentric tendency is structural to the natural history genre. Conventions based on erudite, distanced and objective description from a human subject are designed to enhance the authority of the genre as factual *and* the authority of scientific knowledge systems. However, in many sequences in *After the Fires*, the reality being described is overwhelming. Ecological facts and detached narration cannot contain the affective impacts of acknowledging earth systems in collapse and the catastrophic scale of the losses this is causing. This acknowledgement often prompts emotional responses in narrators, expert and nonexpert. Occasionally, their emotions swamp the screen and generate what Thom Van Dooren and Deborah Bird Rose describe as "ethical witnessing".[15] And it is in these sequences that a very distinctive and moving planetary perspective is realised. In one

---

15 Van Dooren and Rose 2017, 125.

particularly affecting sequence an ecologist, who had been researching wombats for years, is shown returning to a key field site to see if any have survived. The landscape is completely devastated, black, no sign of life. The ecologist describes to camera how any wombats that might still be alive would have retreated deep inside burrows, seeking protection as the fires swept through. They have now been, he says, "left with a world without food or water". When they do venture out, there will be no sustenance. He leaves some food near the entrance to a burrow and then crouches on the ground close to it and starts making plaintive wombat noises: "If she trusts me, she'll come out." A scientist witnessing and mourning loss, desperately calling to a possible animal survivor and drawing audiences into wombat lives.

In Thom Van Dooren and Deborah Bird Rose's schema, ethical witnessing is connected to extinction and loss. It arrives from outside the self, exceeds rational calculation and generates an awareness of "what matters to an other beyond one's own positioning on them".[16] Ethical witnessing acknowledges animal and habitat loss beyond human grief, beyond anthropocentrism. It recognises the diverse ways in which others make and lose their worlds and, in witnessing this, in refusing to turn away, it becomes possible to tell stories about the lives of others in new and consequential ways. The affective micropolitics of some sequences in *After the Fires* evoked many of these ethical effects. They disrupted anthropocentrism and connected animal lives to human lives in ways that suggested care and conversation. These connections went beyond human compassion for threats to the life of other beings or human anticipatory grief about the future. They manifested forms of ethical witnessing that evoked recognition of the interconnected lives of all earthly beings and a sense of shared vulnerability.

This example of ethical witnessing is an important element in generating a sense of planet. The wombat sequence in which an ecologist gets down to ground level in order to communicate with an animal, literally and metaphorically displaced a human perspective and scale and evoked humility and an awareness of mutual interdependence. If a new earth and ecological paradigm is emerging,

---

16   Van Dooren and Rose 2017, 125.

then finding an affinity with others who are affected and developing new alliances is essential. These alliances decentre the normalisation of human "impacts" on nature or environments and the privileging of human knowledge systems. While human responsibility for the Anthropocene as a universal planetary condition might be acknowledged, so too is *diminished* human agency in the face of unpredictable, uneven and insistent planetary forces that cannot be controlled.

Another more significant element in the sense of planet developed in *After the Fires* is an implicit concern about the future of life on earth. Although the program doesn't venture into bleak assessments of the end of the world – apocalyptic thinking never does well on prime-time television – it does examine the fires as evidence of a changing and complex dynamic that is bearing on all life, not just localised contexts.[17] References to the Pyrocene in the program signal that human use of fires and the burning of fossil fuels has become unbounded, triggering fire-catalysed climate change and a new geologic epoch.[18] Like the Anthropocene, the Pyrocene puts human actions at the centre of the story and forces humans to face a difficult truth: human agency has outstripped its capacity to manage itself. Human pretensions to mastery and control are shattered by an earth that is dynamic and volatile, often in ways that are not necessarily caused directly or indirectly by human actions but which offer no immunity to any living thing.

For Cary Wolfe, these escalating and complex new dynamics are planetarity in action and understanding them requires what he terms an "ecologization of the biopolitical paradigm".[19] By this he means a *de*naturalisation of ecologies or a disruption of the equation of ecology with nature. A denaturalised understanding of ecologies investigates forms and patterns through which system and environment relationships are stabilised and managed by forces that are exponentially greater and more complex than any one element in the relationship may possess. The issue for Wolfe is how changing forms

---

17   Wolfe 2017, 218.
18   Pyne 2021.
19   Wolfe 2017, 218.

and patterns emerge and gain increasing power over life. If the Pyrocene, then, is a new pattern, how is it reshaping life?

In outlining the elemental force of the 2019 fires, *After the Fires* explains that the history of fires in Australia is "extreme" but also relatively stable and normal. Fire patterns have shaped nature and culture, but with the eruption of the most savage fire season in the country's history, in which "the whole continent felt like it was on fire", all life is under siege. In describing the catastrophic loss of whole animal cultures, documenting the disappearance of virtually all insects in fire-ravaged areas, explaining how temperate forests cannot cope with constant major fire events because they don't have time to recover and regenerate, the program shows how the planet's ability to reorganise and recover is severely compromised. The implication of this new reality is that environments are not being "shaped" by fires, they are being obliterated by them. A planetary limit has been reached.

To counter this bleak assessment, the program features uplifting sequences on various forms of animal rescue, new forest growth, the survival of a few remaining animals in a threatened species, and conservation strategies based on restoration ecology such as the creation of animal sanctuaries and "insurance populations", as one ecologist interviewed on screen describes them. The message is that life and natural resilience go on. However, even with these sequences, much of the content is about death. If the planetary was once about the unique behaviour of whole self-organising systems and the inherent stabilisation of life – the Gaia thesis – it now appears to be about disequilibrium and death.

This shift in understanding the agency of planetary forces has been played out in Attenborough's Planet programs. In the Blue Planet series, for example, *Blue Planet II* (BBC, 2017) offers a stark warning about the future, quite unlike the first series where equilibrium (which equates with life) was recognised as fragile but enduring. In *After the Fires* there is an undercurrent of anxiety about the ability of the earth to be able to manage new elemental forces like uncontrollable wildfires. In explaining wildfire in implicitly planetary terms, the program effectively ecologised biopolitics. The fires' force and impacts were exceptional and uncontrollable and the irrecoverable losses it created threatened all forms of life. Despite all the images in the program of human care and human acts of rescue and salvation, there was an overwhelming sense that humans were not the exception or master species with solutions. They were part of the "earthly multitudes",[20] dependent on a host of other lives and bodies to live, and as vulnerable to environmental volatility as everything else.

This planetary perspective displaced usual framings of "nature" in natural history. Throughout its evolution, the form has long sought to establish nature and the natural environment as other to culture but knowable and representable. Even when natural environments are recognised as highly *un*natural due to human activities and intervention, nature still stands as the stable referent and contrast to culture. A sense of planet makes this nature/culture distinction impossible to sustain. These fires were more than a "natural disaster"; their localised environmental destruction could not be contained by this framing or spatial context, they were a planetary event. And this event highlighted planetary agency as a radical form of alterity that was both irreducible and indifferent.[21]

Reef Live: Life as a media event

After the Fires examined a catastrophic planetary event through a reflective and expository natural history documentary. It looked back in time and evaluated the fires' impacts and what their intensification means for the future. In contrast, the actual eruption and extensive spread of the fires was covered exhaustively, and often live, by national and global news sources. However, while the fires may have been the lead news item, they also seemed like just another event for disenchanted audiences to absorb in a steady stream of climate-related disasters. News is driven by events, but it can also render them banal. Specially staged, highly promoted live media events are another case altogether. They connect a distinct occurrence in the world to audiences in real time. Royal weddings and Olympic Games, for example, are media events that highlight the complex relations between mediation

---

20 Clark and Szerszynski 2020.
21 Boetzkes 2021.

and the social. It is impossible to understand these events *outside* their mediation, which is so profoundly implicated in ordering and shaping popular experience of them that distinctions between static categories like "the media" and society become meaningless.[22]

In their book *Life After New Media*, Sarah Kember and Joanna Zylinska develop a radical analysis of the centrality and performativity of mediation.[23] Their approach resonates with our argument and extends it in valuable ways. Kember and Zylinska foreground the liveliness of mediation and the ways in which it shapes the unfolding of a media event. They are particularly interested in understanding how live media events involve dynamic forms of mediation that can foreground the shared vitality of media and the world. How, then, does the unfolding of a natural event become a media event? What happens when it is beamed into living rooms, when a direct material connection across space and time is established between nature, media and audiences? And how does this process of mediation shape perceptions of the planet?

This brings us to *Reef Live* (Northern Pictures, 2020), a two-part program in the Your Planet series featuring live-streamed underwater footage of the annual coral spawning on the Great Barrier Reef. Like *After the Fires*, the program was made by Northern Pictures, one of Australia's most successful independent natural history production companies. Production funding came from Screen Australia in association with Screen Queensland, and the program was developed and produced in association with the ABC. Directed by Karina Holden, a conservation biologist by training and Head of Factual Content at Northern Pictures, *Reef Live* was a huge logistical undertaking, involving 120 crew members broadcasting from five locations spread over 1,500 kilometres. "Liveness" was a major point of distinction and featured heavily in the marketing for the program. Holden wanted the audience to witness coral spawning "live in their living rooms, almost like a sporting event". Her objective was to develop innovative approaches to storytelling in relation to the reef that would find new

---

22 Kember and Zylinska 2012, 30.
23 Kember and Zylinska 2012.

audiences and create "co-viewing experiences".[24] The synopsis in the press kit described the program like this:

> A cast of young marine explorers take us on an immersive journey into the frenzy of life on the reef, during a summer of love. Featuring stunning footage of coral spawning, fish breeding, birds and turtles returning to islands to nest, we celebrate the reef *at a time of renewal.*[25]

However, even in this atmosphere of anticipation and excitement about seeing nature "at a time of renewal", the program could not avoid discussing the impacts of planetary changes on the climate and the decline in coral reefs around the world due to bleaching and ocean warming. In a series of diverse pre-recorded sequences, that actually formed the bulk of the content, the reef was represented as an exceptional and vulnerable environment. Home to over 9,000 different species and a huge biodiversity of corals, it was also seriously threatened and the focus of several major scientific projects to support and save it. Reef *life*, it appeared, needed significant technological and scientific help to adapt to a new planetary reality.

These pre-recorded factual sequences about the history, science and fate of the reef were interspersed with live crosses to underwater "reef reporters" ready and waiting for the spawning. The promise of seeing the spawning happen underpinned the unfolding narrative of the program and amplified its central objective: to make a natural event into a media event. On-air promotions appealed to audiences to tune in for a remarkable once-in-a-lifetime experience predicted to happen during the program but with no guarantees. This element of uncertainty – would nature perform on cue? – added to the excitement and suspense, fuelling the sense of a shared experience outside the mundane rituals of normal viewing. It also generated a very different experience of inhabiting a planet. While *After the Fires* struggled to promote nature and life as resilient on a warming planet, *Reef Live* celebrated them thanks to the dynamics of co-present immediacy and

---

24   Northern Pictures 2021, 5.
25   Northern Pictures 2021, 1 (our emphasis).

direct witnessing made possible by live television. Coral reef spawning is a major reproductive occurrence, a spectacular underwater process that occurs in a very limited time period *if* the environmental conditions are right.

Reef Live framed this process as television *and* nature coming together to reveal the renewal of life. Obviously, the coral spawning would have gone on without television, but its presence rearticulated and transformed it in complex ways. Media didn't represent the spawning, they were a productive and generative element in its emergence as an "underwater event like no other".

Celebrations of the possibilities of television and the technical complexities involved in screening the natural event were an ongoing part of the narration. Early in the first episode Hamish Macdonald, the lead host, explained to the audience that "no CGI [computer-generated imagery] was involved in what you are about to see". The other two hosts, Brooke Satchwell and Dr Jordan Nguyen, seated next to Macdonald in front of a huge fish tank in Cairns Aquarium, nodded along and amplified this message with comments like: "yes – this is real", a subtle critique of the use of simulation and stock footage in so much natural history content. This reflexive on-air chatter didn't just acknowledge the central role of technology and mediation in natural history television (much like the making-of documentaries explored in Chapter 4), it also celebrated mediation's dynamic force, its capacity to enter into the world and call it forth in new and exciting ways. Live television promised audiences immersive viewing that would allow them to experience the reef in remarkable ways that were only possible thanks to mediation.

The interactions between the live media event and nature as life are central to the sense of planet that *Reef Live* generated. But what were these interactions and how did they generate distinct perceptions of the reef spawning as a planetary process? How did *Reef Live* reveal the liveliness of nature *and* mediation? How did various sequences in the programs generate an immersive connection with the world that disrupted familiar habits of mind and distinctions like subject–object or nature–culture? And how does turning natural reproduction into a public media event generate tensions between planetary spectacle and planetary decline? These questions displace many of the usual approaches to live events within media studies. The familiar critique of live transmission is that media only *appear* to be live. While the effect may be of direct unmediated access and immediacy with events in the world, the technical process is actually driven by intense artificiality. What happens on screen is highly calculated and formatted by the media apparatus. This critique is built on the assumption that mediation generates a layer or interface between the world and the medium that inevitably masks the real. Or to put it differently, live media can never access real life.

Kember and Zylinska acknowledge this critique, but they are interested in developing a different approach to the live/life tension.[26] If mediation is transformative and productive, if it is a process that orders the world as it calls it into being, then mediation, in their schema, can be seen as another term for "life", for being-in and emerging-with the world.[27] The issue then becomes how to understand the life or vitality of media. How can we understand the processes whereby mediation becomes entangled with the world and helps produce it? This is ultimately a temporal question. Drawing on Henri Bergson,[28] Kember and Zylinska argue that life, like mediation, is synonymous with time, movement and creative evolution. Comprehending time depends on intuition, or processes whereby the sense of movement of our duration is connected to a wider one: "we are able to connect by recognizing our relationality with that which we perceive or observe".[29] For Bergson, experiencing duration as relationality is an exception and often emerges from intuitive knowledge that is very different from intellectual or abstract ways of knowing. Intuitive knowledge can be metaphorical, analogical or imagistic and involves an opening out to the other.[30]

The questions for generating a planetary perspective, then, are: How does witnessing a natural event have the potential to generate intuitive modes of knowledge? Is this dependent on liveness or on modes of mediation and observation that allow the viewer to

---

26 Kember and Zylinska 2012.
27 Kember and Zylinska 2012, 23.
28 Bergson 1944.
29 Kember and Zylinska 2012, 25.
30 Kember and Zylinska 2012, 26.

apprehend the time of the world and their relation to it? Actuality content or live streams are often framed not as representations of the world but as revelations. In this framing, mediation is understood as a mechanism for making things transparently available. This was very much the premise and promise of *Reef Live*. In the first episode there was a lot of build-up from the three-person live "studio" panel seated in Cairns Aquarium. This panel and location grounded the program in the present – panellists spoke directly to camera about what the audience was about to see, introduced pre-recorded sequences and, like all good TV presenters, filled in time by chatting among themselves when the event didn't eventuate when expected. There was lots of anticipatory chatter between them: "tonight is going to be a special night on the Great Barrier Reef"; "this is one of the greatest natural phenomenon on this planet"; "we're all here to see an incredible natural wonder"; "the reef is bursting with new life"; "the coral's biological clocks have to align with various environmental cues"; "all this life bursting out in front of you"; "it's pretty rare to be able to put something like this on television". This commentary was designed to prime the audience, to generate excitement about what was about to happen. It was central to making it into a televisual event, not simply through the use of hyperbole and the usual tactics of talking things up but by aligning the time and experience of viewing with the time of the reef and its biological processes. The temporality generated could be described as an extreme form of presentism: all that matters is now; direct address and direct observation generates a compulsion for immediacy.

To satisfy this compulsion, there were frequent live crosses to underwater scientist commentators observing the coral, assessing its state and the imminence of the spawning event. Talking through specially miked scuba masks, they gave lots of descriptions of how spawning happens and lots of close-ups of coral, but there was no visible spawning. In Episode 1 the spawning event didn't happen. The huge media apparatus in place waiting and watching had to yield to the temporality of the reef and the spawning's unfolding and accept that it wasn't going to occur in prime time. TV's promise of spectacle, of capturing reef time was exceeded by the natural event. Rather than affirming the generative relation between mediation and nature, these sequences seemed to amplify their autonomy and separation: the media waiting to capture and reveal the world but not part of its becoming. The effect of liveness was produced largely through the studio panel chat, not through a sense of the liveliness of mediation. The reef remained an informational object, framed by extensive expository forms of knowledge: scientific facts, history, data and descriptions – but the potentiality of mediation to generate a sense of shared vitality with it was not realised.

Episode 2 realised this potential, but it had little to do with live crosses on television. In the few days in between the screening of Episode 1 and Episode 2, the spawning of the branching corals occurred. When Episode 2 began, Hamish Macdonald announced that: "as predicted, the coral has been spawning right on cue". He then described how camera operators had been filming frantically over the weekend and had captured extraordinary footage that had been live streamed on the ABC's *Reef Live* website. In media event terms, the spawning was made for the endless time of the internet, not the tightly scheduled time of television. However, even with this discrepancy the event talk continued: "the world's biggest breeding event on the planet and it's also the first time in history that we have attempted to broadcast this live on television across the nation"; "it's almost a 'made for television' event". After a few minutes of this studio patter, there was a cut to aerial footage of the coral slick generated by the spawning stretching kilometres down the coast. Brooke Satchwell narrated this footage. She commented on the incredible scale and timing of this event and exclaimed: "the world's largest living structure made up of billions of tiny coral polyps has timed the release of their eggs and sperm perfectly for prime-time broadcasting!" Even though she acknowledged that the footage had been recorded that morning, the claim that the coral polyps had timed their spawning perfectly for television amplified the effect of liveness as an experience of direct witnessing. However, it was the framing and mode of observation that the sequence generated that had an impact far more than the awe-filled narration.

Suddenly the viewer was wrenched out of the studio, and the sense of cosy co-present intimacy with Brooke, into an incredible aerial view of the ocean covered in a white slick snaking along the coastline. Clouds drifted by as the slick made beautiful patterns on the water surface, varying shades of blueness indicating different ocean depths. The scale of this footage was reminiscent of satellite imagery, vast and beyond human modes of perception and visual capacity. The centrality of a human observer and human scale was completely displaced. Zooming out detached humans from the scene but also reinscribed them as scopic masters with seemingly infinite transcendent vision. Time also seemed to be reconfigured – the footage had a cosmological effect, generating a sense of deep time not just live time.

These visual effects have been extensively analysed, particularly in terms of their impact on shaping environmental awareness. The rise of earth imaging and "big optics"[31] has contributed to a major cultural shift in ways of seeing and knowing the "whole earth". Images of the earth seen from outside, whether from space exploration or GPS weather satellites or defence technologies, don't simply displace embodied, earthbound senses of the world and celebrate the power of technical vision, they also generate a very different experience of inhabitation based on connectedness to earth rather than to place or nation.[32] For Heise, these ways of imaging and knowing earth have been fundamental to a sense of planet, but for others they are part of an anthropocentric arrogance that removes humans from the scene and from responsibility. Natural history television has been implicated in this negative assessment. Aerial views, zooming out, exemplify "the God trick", as Donna Haraway calls it,[33] a perspective that generates a sense of observing everything from nowhere and creating a disembodied and universal truth. These techniques are used extensively and have been equated with the visual conquest of nature. Spectacular and seemingly infinite vision has contributed to the visual excess of the genre and the rapacious audience desire to see more and more, all from the comfort of the living room. For Stacy Alaimo, the effect of these endemic practices is to externalise and objectify the planet and ignore how humans have become planetary forces.[34]

The problem with these critiques is that they implicitly privilege the representational logics of media and its effects and marginalise

31 Virilio 1997.
32 Heise 2008.
33 Haraway 1988.
34 Alaimo 2017.

the performative dynamics of mediation. Mediation has been central to making a planetary cultural imaginary. The planet as a cultural force is an outcome of earth imaging; it has emerged in relation with developments in media and imaging technologies, with key institutions from space agencies to the satellite industry and with significant historical events like the moon landing. The interaction of these elements highlights how: "Mediation incorporates technologies and their users, machines and their human counterparts. It is multiagential, and rather than contributing to an interference in history, ... it is contributing to its metamorphosis."[35] The issue is: What distinct processes of mediation made the planetary present in *Reef Live*, and how were humans located and what role did live transmission play?

In their proposal for a multi-scalar approach to time in documentary, Therese Davis and Belinda Smaill explore the potential of environmental documentaries to move beyond an "anthropocentric scale of earth history that privileges human experience ... to show the world as already temporalized in multiple ways".[36] This potential is inherently political, and it could also be understood as inherently planetary. As Davis and Smaill argue, documentary can be a powerful mechanism for understanding and experiencing diverse temporal scales and realities. The ecology of the form, or the way in which it can generate various temporalities and scales of observation that exceed the subject, provokes different regimes of vision and temporal perspectives untethered from the human. Duration is central to this ecological potential in documentary. Like Kember and Zylinska (2012),[37] Davis and Smaill draw on Bergson[38] to develop a multi-scalar approach to duration that recognises the possibility of various temporal scales existing simultaneously, not just in the world but on screen. The issue for environmental documentary is: Which durations are privileged and which are excluded or marginalised?

The coral slick sequence created modes of observation that could be considered as planetary in a number of different registers. These

---

35 Kember and Zylinska 2012, 68.
36 Davis and Belinda Smaill 2018, 20.
37 Kember and Zylinska 2012.
38 Bergson 1944.

modes challenge the critique of earth imaging as fundamentally anthropocentric. While they generated a spatial separation of the viewer from the world spread out below, the temporalities in play made powerful connections possible. The sequence confirmed Davis and Smaill's claim that documentary can reveal how the world is already temporalised in diverse ways.[39] While the slick was a limited biological event, a surface formation occurring in the present, its patterning and relationship to the ocean, coastline and sky drew attention to its interconnections with a vast spatial and temporal scale that exceeded this moment. The aerial perspective amplified this sense of different temporalities interacting: the biological time of the spawning (the slick providing visible evidence of its recent happening) and the expansive time of the reef as an enduring historical environment existing outside and beyond human time.

This perspective also highlighted the fact of mediation, the necessary involvement of a drone or a plane and sophisticated camera technologies to make it all possible. However, "making it possible" did not mean that the media apparatus was constructing this sequence in the sense of distorting or misrepresenting the world. Rather, experiencing these more-than-human temporal and spatial scales foregrounded the performative possibilities of mediation, its generative and transformative dynamics. The promise of the live media event, of seeing nature happen, was displaced by an experience of the liveliness of "mediatic operations".[40] Mediation was revealed as a process that emerged with and ordered the world, that called into being a unique vision of multiple planetary temporalities.

In *Reef Live*, the reef as a local *and* planetary environment was made present in ways that amplified natural history television's attraction to spatial display, spectacle and technical virtuosity, its commitment to revealing everything for the viewer. But the temporalities generated in various "live" sequences complicated these codes and effects. The experience of different temporal scales interacting disrupted the effect of liveness and transparency by making it seem just that: an effect of the present. Meanwhile, infinite oceanic

---

39 Davis and Smaill 2018.
40 Davis and Smaill 2018, 25.

vistas generated a sense of the flow of the world going on regardless before and after the spawning. The event of the spawning may have been televised almost "as it happened", but it was the durational force of the images of the ocean from above, the sense of the world unfolding through time uncontained by the media apparatus, that was most powerful. For viewers, the sequence was almost hypnotic. Exposition and facts gave way to an intuitive and affective encounter with images that were almost abstract, that provoked a different way of knowing and opening to the temporalities of the planet. Zooming out, being separated, did not inhibit connection to planetary being, it enabled it.

The dynamics at work in this aerial sequence confirm Kember and Zylinska's account of mediation as a vital process.[41] This vitality doesn't emerge from television's capacity for liveness or for showing life. Life cannot be known to the intellect, only intuited through experiences that allow the viewer to sense how the movement of their duration is connected to a wider one.[42] When mediation provokes these experiences, when it enters into a productive entanglement with the world that enables a sense of interaction and different awareness, its liveliness is revealed.

Another sequence in *Reef Live* shows this process at work in a very different way. Rather than creating modes of observation driven by big optics, this sequence offered an underwater immersive experience. Crossing to a reef reporter, the viewer was transported into water's unique movement, its drift and primordial locomotion. The sense of being suspended in a dynamic fluid environment surrounded by corals, fish, seaweed and the ocean was powerful. Then the camera zoomed in for an extreme close-up of a polyp releasing its egg. The narrator, speaking through his scuba mask, framed the footage in terms of the miracle of nature renewing itself. As the camera pulled back, a huge drift of eggs swirling through the water "like snow" was visible. The narrator exclaimed that he "was in an absolute storm of life ... this is like watching a galaxy being born before your eyes!" The promise from the studio hosts to take the audience "inside the event" seemed to be realised. In contrast to the vast horizontal expanse of the ocean viewed

---

41 Kember and Zylinska 2012.
42 Kember and Zylinska 2012, 25.

from above, the view from inside generated a sense of trans-corporeal merging, of inhabiting the reef viscerally. Water is a mediator: entering it and becoming immersed generates unique experiences of embodiment or disembodiment. This sequence captured that sense of merging with or dissolving into the immediate environs, becoming fluid thanks to underwater cameras and the overwhelming force of water's liquid materiality. As we have argued, time is central to mediation and here the temporal scale generated was of intense immediacy, dissolving into the present world. This temporality may be enhanced by appeals to witnessing a live natural event, but it does not depend on it. Presentism is different from live: it is an experience of duration that amplifies the time of now, being incorporated into the movement of the world, being with *and* in biological time. Zooming in, going underwater made a different sense of planet possible. The immersive dissolve of the subject and human scale made interacting living systems visible: fish, plants, corals, water, all interconnected and interacting.

Conclusion

After the Fires (Northern Pictures, 2020) and *Reef Live* (Northern Pictures, 2020) are evidence of important shifts in the political and ethical possibilities of natural history programs. While they deployed many of the standard cultural codes – the resilience of nature, the role of science in helping it adapt, the impacts of humans on the environment, the beauty and vulnerability of animals and natural systems – they also opened up new approaches and critical themes. The most significant was the generation of planetary framings and perspectives. These framings are by no means new to the genre; as Attenborough has shown, they now drive much of the production focus for shows targeting global markets. Animals inhabiting a planet and dependent on vast interconnected ecological and geophysical processes like the climate are far more exportable than those contained by national or local environments. These programs amplified these framings, but they also gave them distinct and powerful inflections by foregrounding what it means to inhabit a damaged planet.

After the Fires contained powerful sequences of animal loss and landscape devastation that generated moments of profound ethical witnessing. Inhabiting, here, meant acknowledging planetary forces at work in mass animal death. It also meant responding to this reality beyond human grief and anthropocentrism. By witnessing the diverse ways in which others make and lose their worlds, by refusing to turn away, *After the Fires* showed how it was possible to tell stories about the lives of animals and landscapes in new and consequential ways. The affective micropolitics of some sequences in *After the Fires* evoked ethical effects that disrupted anthropocentrism and connected animal lives to human lives in ways that suggested mutual implication in planetary forces beyond control.

Reef Live played with the dynamics of the live media event to stage coral spawning as a landmark television experience. But it was the liveliness of mediation that was more significant: the generative and transformative dynamics of mediation calling forth a reef that allowed viewers to experience the multiple temporalities of planetary life, to inhabit it in an immersive encounter. These natural history programs made the planet palpable by exploring its myriad spatial and temporal scales, its agency as an immutable force and the impacts of destructive human activity. The idea of science to the rescue, of natural adaptation and resilience – for so long natural history stand-bys – seemed difficult to promote. The senses of planet generated were complex, affecting and often very hard to witness. Inhabiting a damaged planet makes for provocative and often difficult viewing.

Conclusion
Political animals

What has it meant to make animals public on the ABC and what have been the social and political effects of this? In exploring this question, the assumption that animals were simply instrumental in the realisation of public service broadcasting, passive objects recruited to facilitate the political objectives of educating, informing and entertaining audiences, was resisted. Instead, we have explored how animals were made into "devices of the public", how the myriad practices of making animals public – of visualising and accounting for them in various ways – provoked new forms of public interest and engagement and new forms of political entanglement, good and bad.

Our primary focus has been the natural history animal which, as we have shown, manifests a very distinct and shifting form of televisual animality. Incarcerated in a media environment, these animals have continuously evolved and animated human–nonhuman relations in ways that both reflected and shaped wider cultural figurations. If culture and technique are central to animality, as Dominique Lestel and colleagues argue,[1] then the sociotechnical practices of television and the changing institutional cultures of the ABC, as a powerful national communication infrastructure, were central to configuring the performances of natural history animals. Situating them in nature or

---

1   Lestel, Bussolini and Chrulew 2014.

the environment or the national imaginary or the planet, revealing their unique behaviours, narrating their performances and informing audiences about their worlds all shaped their unique modes of televisual being and attached audiences to them.

But what of the animals themselves? In what ways did they resist or embrace the complexities of becoming public and the demands of attracting audience attention and interest? This was a harder question to answer because the archive offered only fleeting insights into animal realities before they made it to the screen. And when those realities were described, they were mediated by the particular modes of inscription used to represent them, for example: the camera operator's field notes or the inter-office memo explaining how wombats survived a flight interstate for filming. While making-of documentaries, such as the one explored in Chapter 4, promised to show all, to reveal the real animal behind the screen animal, this was a false promise. This format, just like all others, contained and provoked animals according to very specific conventions. Of course, animals are never fully disciplined by these conventions: their bodies actively shape meaning and often determine what is filmed and how. However, recognising the expressive force of the animal body does not diminish the fact that yearning to get to the authentic animal is very problematic. It fuels assumptions about representations and their relationship to the real that implicitly devalue the force and vitality of mediated animals.

We have rejected the real/unreal opposition or the equation of "constructed" with "fake" by shifting from a representational idiom to a performative one. This approach foregrounded how televisual animals were incited or provoked and how they depended on specific fields of reference or accountability relations about what counted as credible in a televisual setting. The ABC had to create forms of realism that enabled audiences to feel comfortable with the natural history animals it broadcast, to be willing to accept their televisual performances as evidence of animals' unique modes of being. For, as Derek Bousé insists, realism is about *plausibility* not accuracy; it's about a relation to reality, not direct correlation.[2] The idea of provocation made it possible to investigate this relation and examine how the techniques and event

---

2   Bousé 2000, 8.

Conclusion

of televisual capture brought forth ABC animals. It also made it possible to acknowledge the pull of these mediated animals; their capacity to be affecting, not just informative or entertaining. The critical point our empirical analysis confirmed was that natural history animals weren't so much found and documented as provoked and enacted.

What then of the impacts of these televisual natural history animals that have roamed ABC screens for decades? The other side to provocation is the capacity to be provocative, to pose questions to audiences, to generate social and political effects. One of the key issues we have been concerned with is whether televisual animals have constrained or extended political and ethical involvement with animals and environments. Making animals public did not automatically make them political; it did not necessarily invite progressive engagement with them. In many instances, making animals public in the ABC had anti-political effects in the sense that it either reinforced human sovereignty or established a clear boundary between animal and human or limited the possibility of ethical complexity and engagement. How the ABC made animals political is connected to the dynamics of publicness, but it is also distinct from those dynamics. The public and the political are not synonymous.[3] Understanding the connections between making animals public and making them political involves an investigation of how provoking and explaining animals that are real can also allow them to *become provocative*. As Vinciane Despret points out, when describing the work of ethologists and scientists in explaining animal worlds: "there are explanations which end up multiplying worlds and celebrating the emergence of an infinite number of modes of existence and others which seek to impose order, bringing them back to a few basic principles".[4]

Despret's distinction between *multiplying* worlds and modes of existence or *ordering* them is central to the political provocations of natural history animals. There is no question that making animals public on the ABC changed how audiences understood the lives of animals and their worlds. However, it wasn't just animal worlds that were revealed and explained but also human worlds and their relation

---

3   Warner 2002.
4   Despret 2022, 6.

to or implication in animal modes of existence. The question is: How were human–animal relationships ordered in natural history television? In investigating how ABC animals were crafted, we were not only interested in how they performed but for whom and with what consequences. In what ways did these animal performances shape the identity of their observers and the nature of human–animal interactions? Did natural history animals invite audiences to watch as sovereign humans, as concerned publics, as viewers expecting to be entertained, as environmental citizens or as companions in a multispecies encounter? Did the way natural history animals were accounted for position the audience as observers gaining access to an exotic world of others? Or did it multiply worlds by removing humans from the centre of the story and acknowledging diverse and entangled modes of existence?

These questions signal the political implications of provoking natural history animals. In our analysis we sought to understand how ABC animals became enrolled in political and public life. We were interested in how animals' capacities to be provocative emerged. This involved empirical investigations of the processes whereby various concerns came to qualify ABC animals, making them into political issues and sometimes political actors. As we have noted, this was not an inevitable process. Many ABC animals did not provoke political questions or ethical anxieties in viewers. Many were framed in ways that actively denied wider political realities or that configured politics as an exclusively human activity utterly remote from the timeless other world of nature and animals. Animals roaming in purified natures free of base human conflicts or gross abuse or environmental degradation are examples of this. What this diversity of representations and political concerns signals is that ABC animals were not *essentially* political, this framing and qualification had to be enacted – the issue is how: what techniques made animals into political objects or subjects? How did they become implicated in provoking various issues and concerns, in posing questions to audiences? In insisting that politics are emergent and performative, we were less concerned with abstract critiques of animal–human relations and more focused on empirically documenting the ways in which mediated animals came to deny or display political potency, and the myriad ways in which humans became entangled with them.

Approaches committed to investigating exactly how political animals emerge are often opposed to the practice of critique. Within critical animal studies, for example, there is extensive analysis of animal exploitation and the uneven power relations between humans and animals. The assumption is that critique is foundational to effective political analysis and incompatible with investigations of politics as process, as situated enactment. Our concern with critique was that, in the rush to assess mediated animals as evidence of essentially exploitative modes of vision, the diversity of ABC animals and the various political engagements they provoked could be overlooked. Critique makes it difficult to see how some natural history animals might be generative of changed and better human–animal relations, how they might provoke positive multispecies encounters. In our examination of animals on the ABC, we investigated *how* political concerns emerged or were excluded in making these animals public. The questions we wrestled with were: What properties and realities of animals became potent in the processes of provoking wildlife realities on TV and how were these properties configured as political? How were human–animal relations qualified by ethical concerns?

In shifting from notions of representation and critique to performance and provocation, we investigated the ways in which televisual animals reached into the world and activated specific forms of accountability – scientific, aesthetic, ethical and more. These accounts established essential reference points for making animals plausible and compelling, and they generated diverse political effects and affects. While ABC television content was our primary empirical material, we approached this not as a discrete domain of visual representation, not as a body of texts awaiting critical readings, but as material that *realised* and circulated very particular animals and configured a diversity of human–animal relations. If, as Javier Lezaun and colleagues argue: "Provocations are meant to pose a challenge, to ... *reveal a new reality*",[5] how did ABC television as a public institution and visual medium reveal new realities about animals?

---

5   Lezaun, Muniesa and Vikkelsø 2013, 280 (our emphasis).

First, there is no doubt that the ABC gave audiences access to Australian animals and their habitats and revealed new realities about them that had never been seen before on television. While charismatic Australian animals were relatively familiar to viewers, when television commenced "nature" on the small screen was something that happened elsewhere, that was largely imported. As the ABC began making natural history content or its own "nature shows", audiences were able to witness "wild Australia": a generic term first used by the ABC in 1971 that was then used to brand myriad natural history programs over decades. Not the wilds of Africa or Europe or the Americas, but a natural world inhabited by unique Australian animals. Giving audiences access to Australian fauna and flora invoked the logics of the wider exhibitionary complex already in place in zoos and museums. It helped realise the political rationality of public broadcasting by configuring the audience as a population requiring education and information and by enrolling animals in this project. As we saw in Part One, the imperative to "show and tell" in early natural history programs implicitly adjudicated the boundary between human and animal. Humans were there to watch and learn about animals that were captured in a largely self-contained natural world. As significant as the commitment to access was, as important as it was in orienting audiences to Australian animals, it shaped a political disposition that assured these audiences that *they* were sovereign. Early natural history programming configured and confirmed anthropocentrism.

As the Natural History Unit expanded and developed the genre during the 1970s and 80s, ratings grew significantly. The proliferation of content from the NHU during this period built new audiences keen to look at animals as objects of difference, scientific curiosity and natural beauty. Natural history series like *Wild Australia: The Southern Edge* (NHU, 1979), *Exploration North* (NHU, 1978) and *The World We Share* (NHU, 1981), for example, often occupied prime time in the ABC schedule and attracted significant ratings and reviews. These series covered a vast array of content and showed animals and places, in Australia and beyond, that were impossible for audiences to see in any other way. They confirmed to audiences that television was an important and trusted source of information about animals and nature.

Conclusion

Natural history programs during this period were a tribute to the energy and commitment of the small staff in the NHU and their ingenuity in creating co-production partnerships with numerous government and scientific institutions. Some of the content produced was most definitely blue chip in its framing of nature as spectacular and timeless and animals as exotic or charismatic. These shows also often displayed high production values in their drive to realise the natural history animal as a quality beast. Other shows were structured more as expository documentaries illustrating scientific facts or biological processes with an explicit pedagogic intent. In many of the internal discussions within the NHU about program ideas for new productions, there was concern about balancing the ABC's imperative to both inform and entertain. NHU staff were keen to inform, but the demands of television, and the unit's survival in the ABC, often meant that entertainment had to be prioritised. A 1984 report on the activities of the NHU produced by John Vandenbeld, director of the unit at the time, captured this dilemma well: "Given that we have to inform *and* entertain, while allowing that one overlays the other, my interpretation of the various audience surveys is that wildlife programmes are seen primarily as escapist, entertainment fare."[6]

This assessment, that audiences approached natural history programs as escapist entertainment, confirms John Frow's argument about the social force of genre.[7] What audiences came to expect from these shows were animals that would not confront them or disturb their sense of human sovereignty; animals that were performing *for* them; animals whose natural history realities were being displayed *for* them in an entertaining way. Wildlife content was a zone where human–animal difference and hierarchy were firmly established. These patterns of meaning became durable as the genre grew and consolidated. The force of these genre conventions was to generally preclude natural history as a space for complex or uncomfortable political or multispecies encounters.

---

6   John Vandenbeld, Report on NHU for ABC Corporate Planning, 22 June 1984. ABC NHU Archive, Box 12/405.
7   Frow 2006.

However, the demands and force of the natural history genre were also mediated by the wider political rationality of the ABC as a public broadcaster. As noted, the ABC Charter emphasised "informing, educating and entertaining all Australians" as one of its central objectives. This objective didn't just shape the genre conventions of natural history content and animals, it also had governmental effects. Making entertaining content that appealed to audiences and generated good ratings was an immediate goal essential to the survival of the NHU. However, beyond this was another set of expectations about what the natural history animal was supposed to do. These expectations configured the animal as a device for making *citizens* not just ratings. Capturing animal performances that informed audiences about their nation and its unique nature and ecologies was central to the emergence of the NHU, as we saw in Chapter 2 and the accounts justifying the unit's creation in 1973. Ten years later this governmental function for the Natural History Unit remained strong. As Vandenbeld argued:

> We regard the production of quality natural history programmes as one of the TV Features department's most important activities. It deals with the fundamental issue of the *nation's relationship with its environment* ... Australians' future well-being will depend on the decisions they make about the kind of environment they want to have, and the way they want to manage it. Such decisions can only be effective if they are informed ones, based on understanding and knowledge of the forces at work around them.[8]

In this explanation of the governmental role of the NHU, the natural history animal didn't just live in nature or Australia, it lived in "the environment"; and it was incumbent on audiences to be informed about and manage this environment, to understand the "forces at work around them". Environments were not timeless purified zones, they were complex spaces significantly transformed by human and economic interventions.

---

8   John Vandenbeld, Report on NHU for ABC Corporate Planning, 22 June 1984 ABC NHU Archive, Box 12/405 (our emphasis).

Conclusion

Natural history content that explored the relations between animals and the environment increased significantly during the 1980s. This was undoubtedly a response to the growth of environmental movements during the 1970s in Australia but also, perhaps, due to a certain exhaustion with the limitations of some natural history genre conventions. A review of an episode in *The World We Share* (NHU, 1983) series, which focused on Gippsland, captured this sense of exhaustion like this:

> Perhaps we've been spoiled by too many excellent nature documentaries but the Gippsland edition of Channel 2's *The World We Share* is not exciting viewing ... Without wanting to sound blasé about nature's miracles, we have seen most of these scenes before – only the location is different.[9]

The invocation of "the environment" created a way out of this impasse: same old nature, different location. Relocating animals into *environments* meant that animal modes of existence multiplied, and an array of different issues could be introduced into natural history programs. More critically, it meant that animals could now be provocative; they could pose questions about human impacts and exploitation. Beyond access – with its problematic anthropocentric effects – the second significant impact of natural history programs has been their influence on developing environmental awareness in audiences. While this influence is impossible to quantify, there is no question that many natural history programs on the ABC revealed a significant political commitment to both exploring and legitimising a wide range of environmental issues. These programs also addressed audiences as being implicated in these issues in various ways: as concerned subjects, as advocates, as threats. In this way, natural history programming played a critical role in the formation of environmental citizens. Of course, there were many other institutions that were equally influential in developing environmental awareness and advocacy in

---

9   TV review of the "Gippsland" episode of *The World We Share* series (NHU, 1983). Titled "Micro-country", author Mark Lawrence (no date, no source). ABC NHU Archive, Box 12/405.

populations, but natural history programming on the ABC was a very significant and important force. It encouraged audiences to engage with "the environment" as a matter of concern, as warranting civic attention not just curiosity.[10] Watching these programs in the privacy of the home was an experience of individualised media consumption *and* collective political engagement. Natural history programs reflected wider public debates about the decline of the environment and offered viewers mediated forms of participation in them. It invited them to watch as active citizens not just entertainment hungry consumers.

Programs that were focused on environmental issues often examined difficult human–animal realities, such as: feral populations and how to manage them; returning injured animals to the wild; the work of scientists in trying to save threatened species; and damaged landscapes and their ecologies. Their central logic was problematisation or the generation of issues and ethical quandaries about animals and environments. In "Kinchega: Under New Management", an episode from the 1983 series *The World We Share* (NHU, 1983), the NHU worked with the New South Wales Parks and Wildlife Service to document the struggle to turn a degraded sheep farm into a national park and restore its ravaged ecology. Since the sheep had gone, the kangaroo population had rapidly expanded to the point where these iconic animals now posed a threat to the survival of other vulnerable native species. The central dilemma driving the program and put to audiences was: Is it time to cull the kangaroo population and how should this be done? Equally problematic were the large and very destructive feral pig populations that had to be eradicated using shooters in helicopters. The "environment" in this program was damaged and vulnerable with a complex history of colonial intervention and gross economic exploitation. As the rangers interviewed on screen noted, the idea of restoring Kinchega back to some mythical pristine natural state was virtually impossible.

"Kinchega" problematised the complexities of conservation and represented animals as the target of human killing, not just objects of display or protection. The culling of kangaroos was justified in the name of ecological protection and implicitly educated viewers about

---

10   Latour 2005b.

Conclusion

the work of environmentalists. Contrast this to the culling of kangaroos in *The Trail of the 'Roo*, which was examined in Chapter 1. In that 1930s film, the death of animals was linked to pastoral economic growth and functioned as a form of entertainment for audiences, not education.

Concerns and ethical dilemmas about culling and conservation did not entirely dominate in "Kinchega: Under New Management". The program also included a smattering of natural history spectacle, such as rare dancing snakes and masses of cormorants gathered around waterholes. But the cutaways to shots of helicopters chasing feral pigs and references to "war" somewhat took the edge off these standard natural history conventions and pleasures. What justified these different animal realities and the tensions between them was the advocacy of conservation as a necessary human practice in the interests of protecting and caring for animals and environments. As in other natural history content the narration by Robyn Williams, a well-known ABC science presenter, was implicitly pedagogic with a focus on the ethical and political difficulties of managing animals. Scientific and aesthetic accounts of animals were not entirely displaced, but they were not dominant. What was foregrounded was the political problem of which animals to conserve and how, who belonged and who didn't. Viewers were addressed as environmentally concerned citizens and invited to engage with Kinchega as a site of difficult political decisions but also as a place in need of care. How could conservation as care and protection be enacted without sacrificing some animals for others?

Using natural history as a form of advocacy or environmental awareness extended the types of human–animal engagement in these programs. It pushed audiences into different modes of viewing beyond curiosity or entertainment. Instead, they were invited into multispecies encounters that foregrounded the complexities and politics of human–animal relations. While this content worked on the level of exposition and factual documentary and was attentive to different perspectives, it also worked on affective registers inviting viewers to be moved by the plight of disappearing or vulnerable ecosystems. It was inherently ethical in the way that it foregrounded what it means to care for and conserve nonhuman others that have become endangered because of human actions. This was television that provoked very different natural history animals and very different forms of public interest. Animals weren't just performing for humans, they were posing questions to them. They were provocative, not just provoked.

The displacement of nature with the environment generated more complex social and political effects and forms of engagement. However, even with this displacement and the exploration of a vast array of animals and landscapes in natural history programs throughout the 1990s, nature remained the stable referent. It was resilient and would always go on, with a bit of help from scientists or environmental management. Environmentalism offered a fuller recognition of nature cultures, but it also had certain limits. Controversial issues like climate change were generally avoided or downplayed; humans were both destroyers and rescuers, there to help nature recover and adapt. It wasn't until the rise of a planetary perspective, which we explored in Chapter 6, that the end of nature was contemplated. As we discussed, programs in the Your Planet (ABC, 2020) series could be described as post-natural history. They acknowledged and showed ecological collapse, mass extinctions and the increasing instability of the climate. They also positioned audiences as ethical witnesses to losses that exceeded rational calculation, were outside of human control and provoked recognition of the interconnected lives of all earthly beings and a sense of shared vulnerability. These provocations made for very affecting and at times uncomfortable viewing. To be moved by these televisual animals, to be captured by their performances, to feel the pull of interconnectedness and shared worlds is to open up to the possibility of what Casper Bruun Jensen calls "cosmo-ecological alliances".[11]

This possibility is the final sociopolitical effect or potential we can detect in natural history programs. For Jensen, cosmo-ecological alliances are urgently needed in the face of the Anthropocene. They cannot involve hierarchy, or the ordering of relations that gives god-like status or powers to humanity. Instead, he argues that:

> thinking the new earth must entail learning from a ground-level position (or with) other human and more-than-human actors. In lieu of arrogance, what must be nourished is awareness of mutual interdependencies, and a corresponding sense of humility.[12]

---

11 Jensen 2022.

Conclusion

Recent natural history programs have offered glimpses of this. As we saw in *Reef Live* (Northern Pictures, 2020), the vitality of mediation revealed the vitalism of planetary life from a cosmo-ecological perspective. When the cameras took the audience underwater, the view from inside the ocean generated a sense of trans-corporeal merging, of inhabiting the reef viscerally. As Melody Jue argues, water is a mediator; entering it and becoming immersed generates unique experiences of embodiment or disembodiment.[13] This sequence in *Reef Live* captured the sense of merging with or dissolving into the immediate environs, becoming fluid thanks to the sociotechnical capacities of underwater cameras and the overwhelming force of water's liquid materiality. The temporal scale generated was of intense immediacy, dissolving into the present world. This sequence also framed the ocean as a milieu – not an abstract "environment" out there. A milieu is dynamic and generative, it provokes different sorts of knowledge and different perspectives. Being underwater reorients and disrupts terrestrial points of view; the human is no longer grounded.[14] It also opens up the radical possibility of natural history television: the capacity to disrupt human sovereignty and provoke new mediations and cosmo-ecological alliances.

---

12   Jensen 2022, 39.
13   Jue 2020.
14   Jue 2020, 11.

References

TV programs mentioned

Animal World (NBC, 1968–1971).
Around the Bush with Vincent Serventy (ABC, 1964).
Australia Today (ABC, 1964).
Australian Walkabout (BBC, 1959).
Big Weather: And How to Survive It (Northern Pictures, 2020).
Blue Planet (BBC, 2001).
Bush Quest with Robin Hill (ABC, 1970).
David Attenborough: Extinction (BBC, 2020).
David Attenborough's Conquest of the Skies (Atlantic Productions, 2014).
Dancing Orpheus (ABC, 1962).
Exploration North (ABC NHU, 1978).
Kinchega: Under New Management (ABC NHU, 1983).
Kingdom of the Sea (Emperor Production/Guild Films, 1957–1958).
Lassie (CBS, 1954–1973).
Life on Earth (BBC, 1979).
Look (BBC, 1955–1968).
Nature of Australia: A Portrait of the Island Continent (ABC Natural History Unit, in association with Australian Heritage Commission, BBC Television and WNET/13, 1988).
Our Planet (Netflix, 2019).
Planet Earth (BBC, 2006).

Reef Live (Northern Pictures, 2020).
Skippy the Bush Kangaroo (Fauna Productions, 1968–1970).
The Bird of the Thunderwoman (ABC NHU, 1980).
The Making of David Attenborough's Conquest of the Skies (Colossus Productions, 2014).
The Man Who Loves Frogs (ABC NHU, 1985).
The Shark Hunters (Ron Taylor Productions, 1963).
The Trail of the 'Roo (MCD Productions, 1931).
True Life Adventure (The Walt Disney Company, 1948–1960).
Untamed World (CTV Television Network, 1968–1976).
Where Angels Swim (ABC NHU, 1981).
Wild Australia: After the Fires (Northern Pictures, 2020).
Wild Australia: Beyond the Dunes (ABC, 1972).
Wildfire (ABC NHU, 1980).
Wildlife Australia (ABC/CSIRO, 1962–1964).
Wildlife of Papua New Guinea: "The Immigrant Deer" (ABC NHU, 1975).
Zoo Quest: "Zoo Quest for a Dragon" (BBC, 1956).
Zoorama: San Diego Zoo (CBS, 1955).

ABC documents

ABC NHU Archive, Box 12/4751, Box 11/1427, Box 10/5418, Box 11/5779.
Australian Broadcasting Commission, *Annual Reports*, 1933–1983 Sydney: ABC.
Australian Broadcasting Corporation, *Annual Reports*, 1984–2020. Sydney: ABC.

Books, articles and press kits

Advertiser (1933). The Trail of the 'Roo. Adelaide, 6 January, 2. No author.
Agamben, Giorgio (2004). *The Open: Man and Animal*. Redwood City, CA: Stanford University Press.
Alaimo, Stacy (2017). Your shell on acid: material immersion, Anthropocene dissolves. In Richard Grusin, ed. *Anthropocene Feminism*, 89–120. Minneapolis: University of Minnesota Press.
Anderson, Benedict (1991). *Imagined Communities: Reflections on the Origin and Spread of Nationalism*. London: Verso.
Argus (1927). Kangaroo film: To the Editor of The Argus. Melbourne, 5 November, 29. No author.
Argus (1927). Kangaroo drive. Objections to film. Scenes suggesting cruelty. Melbourne, 18 October, 17. No author.

References

Attenborough, David (1980). *The Zoo Quest Expeditions: Travels in Guyana, Indonesia and Paraguay*. Guildford: Lutterworth Press.

Bagust, Phil (2008). Screen natures: special effects and edutainment in the "new" hybrid wildlife documentary. *Continuum* 22(2): 213–26.

Barad, Karen (2007). *Meeting the Universe Halfway: Quantum Physics and the Entanglement of Matter and Meaning*. Durham, NC: Duke University Press.

Bennett, Brett (2017). Decolonization, environmentalism and nationalism in Australia and South Africa. *Itinerario* 41(1): 27–50.

Bennett, Tony (1995). *The Birth of the Museum: History, Theory, Politics*. London: Routledge.

Bennett, Tony, Pat Buckridge, David Carter and Colin Mercer, eds (2000). *Celebrating the Nation: A Critical Study of Australia's Bicentenary*. London: Routledge.

Berger, John (2009). *Why Look at Animals?* London: Penguin.

Bergson, Henri (1944). *Creative Evolution*. Arthur Mitchell, trans. New York: Random House.

Bhabha, Homi K. (1994). *Location of Culture*. London: Routledge.

Blue, Gwendolyn (2015). Multispecies publics in the Anthropocene: from symbolic exchange to material-discursive intra-action. In HARN Editorial Collective, eds. *Animals in the Anthropocene: critical perspectives on non-human futures*, 165–76. Sydney: Sydney University Press.

Boetzkes, Amanda (2021). Cold sun hot planet: solarity's aesthetic, planetary perspective. *South Atlantic Quarterly* 120(1): 91–102.

Bousé, Derek (2000). *Wildlife Films*. Philadelphia: University of Pennsylvania Press.

Bowker, Geoffrey C. (2010). The ontological priority of mediation. In Madeleine Akrich, Yannick Barthe, Fabien Muniesa and Philippe Mustar, eds. *Débordements: Mélanges offerts à Michel Callon*, 61–8. Paris: Presses des Mines.

Boyde, Melissa (2006). Introduction. In Melissa Boyde, ed. *Captured: The Animal Within Culture*, 1–8. London: Palgrave Macmillan.

Braun, Bruce and Sarah Whatmore, eds (2010). *Political Matter: Technoscience, Democracy and Public Life*. Minneapolis: University of Minnesota Press.

Burt, Jonathan (2002). *Animals in Film*. London: Reaktion Books.

Chow, Rey (2012). *Entanglements, or Transmedial Thinking about Capture*. Durham, NC: Duke University Press.

Chris, Cynthia (2006). *Watching Wildlife*. Minneapolis: University of Minnesota Press.

Clark, Nigel and Bronislaw Szerszynski (2020). *Planetary Social Thought*. Cambridge: Polity Press.

Collard, Rosemary-Claire (2016). Electric elephants and the lively/lethal energies of wildlife documentary film. *Area* 48: 472–79. https://tinyurl.com/27hw722j.

Cook, Ann-Marie (2015). Re-assessing the demise of the McDonagh sisters. *Screening the Past*, August. https://tinyurl.com/45adnmf3.

Cottle, Simon (2004). Producing nature(s): on the changing production ecology of natural history TV. *Media, Culture and Society* 26(1): 81–101.

Couldry, Nick and Andreas Hepp (2016). *The Mediated Construction of Reality*. Cambridge: Polity.

Creed, Barbara (2015). Films, gestures, species. *Journal for Cultural Research* 19(1): 43–55.

Crutzen, Paul (2002). Geology of mankind. *Nature* 415(23). https://tinyurl.com/2r7pfm6s.

Cubitt, Sean (2005). *Eco Media*. Amsterdam and New York: Rodopi.

Davis, Therese and Belinda Smaill (2018). Rethinking documentary and the environment: a multi-scalar approach to time. *Transformations* 32: 19–37.

Despret, Vinciane (2022). *Living as a Bird*. Helen Morrison, trans. Cambridge: Polity.

Despret, Vinciane (2016). *What Would Animals Say If We Asked the Right Questions?* Brett Buchanan, trans. Minneapolis: University of Minnesota Press.

Despret, Vinciane (2004). The body we care for: figures of anthropo-zoo-genesis. *Body and Society* 10(2–3): 111–34.

Dibley, Ben (2020). Capturing spectral beasts: marsupial performances of the cinematic undead. *Australian Humanities Review* 67(1).

Dibley, Ben (2018). Technofossil: a memento mori. *Journal of Contemporary Archaeology* 5(1): 44–52.

Dibley, Ben and Gay Hawkins (2019). Making animals public: early wildlife television and the emergence of environmental nationalism on the ABC. *Continuum: Journal of Media and Cultural Studies* 33(6): 744–58. https://doi.org/10.1080/10304312.2019.1669533.

Dyer, Glenn (2007). The ABC's Natural History Unit becomes history. *Crikey*, 17 August. https://tinyurl.com/ckt3ypjj.

Fisher, Humphrey (1981). Inter-office Memo: Bicentenary Year, 1 April 1981. ABC NHU Archive, Box 12/4751.

Fitzsimons, Trish, Pat Laughren and Dugald Williamson (2011). *Australian Documentary: History, Practices and Genres*. Melbourne: Cambridge University Press.

Frow, John (2006). *Genre*. Abingdon, Oxon: Routledge.

References

Genosko, Gary (2005). Natures and cultures of cuteness. *Invisible Culture: An Electronic Journal for Visual Studies* 9. https://tinyurl.com/3phbmydw.

Ginn, Franklin (2008). Extension, subversion, containment: eco-nationalism and (post)colonial nature in Aotearoa New Zealand. *Transactions of the Institute of British Geographers* 33(3): 335–53.

Gleitzman, Morris (1988). Where reptiles rule. *Sydney Morning Herald*, 1 June.

Gouyon, Jean-Baptiste (2019). *BBC Wildlife Documentaries in the Age of Attenborough*. Switzerland: Palgrave Macmillan.

Gouyon, Jean-Baptiste (2016). "You can't make a film about mice just by going out into a meadow and looking at mice": staging as knowledge production in natural history film-making. In Martin Willis, ed. *Staging Science: Scientific Performances on Street, Stage and Screen*, 83–103. London, UK: Palgrave Macmillan.

Gouyon, Jean-Baptiste (2011). The BBC Natural History Unit: instituting natural history film-making in Britain. *History of Science: Review of Literature* vol. xlix. Cambridge: Science History Publications: 425–51.

Guiler, Eric (1986). The Beaumaris Zoo in Hobart. *Papers and Proceedings of the Tasmanian Historical Research Association* 33(4): 121–71.

Haraway, Donna (2008). *When Species Meet*. Minneapolis: University of Minnesota Press.

Haraway, Donna (1992). *Primate Visions: Gender, Race, and Nature in the World of Modern Science*. New York: Routledge.

Haraway, Donna (1988). Situated knowledges: the science question in feminism and the privilege of a partial perspective. *Feminist Studies* 14(3): 575–99.

Hawkins, Gay (2013). Enacting public value on the ABC's Q&A: from normative to performative approaches. *Media International Australia Incorporating Culture and Policy* 146(1): 82–92.

Hawkins, Gay and Ben Dibley (2020). Provoking animal realities on TV: exploring the affinities between STS and screen studies. *Science, Technology & Human Values* 46(4): 695–718. https://doi.org/10.1177/0162243920945381.

Hawkins, Gay and Ben Dibley (2019). Natural history on TV: how the ABC took Australian animals to the people. *Conversation*, 20 November. https://tinyurl.com/mr2b4h2w.

Hawkins, Gay, Emily Potter and Kane Race (2015). *Plastic Water: The Social and Material Life of Bottled Water*. Cambridge, MA: MIT Press.

Heise, Ursula K. (2008). *Sense of Place and Sense of Planet: The Environmental Imagination of the Global*. Oxford: Oxford University Press.

Hill, Robin (1988). Aunty answers nature's call. *Sydney Morning Herald*, 9 May.

Horak, Jan-Christopher (2006). Wildlife documentaries: from classical forms to reality TV. *Film History* 18(4): 459–75.

Inglis, Kenneth (1983). *This Is the ABC: The Australian Broadcasting Commission 1932-1983*. Melbourne: Melbourne University Press.
Jensen, Casper Bruun (2022). Thinking the new earth: cosmoecology and new alliances in the Anthropocene. *Darshika: Journal of Integrative and Innovative Humanities* 2(1), 26-43.
https://tinyurl.com/5n92p4jr.
Jue, Melody (2020). *Wild Blue Media*. Durhman and London: Duke University Press.
Kember, Sarah and Joanna Zylinska (2012). *Life After New Media*. Cambridge, MA: MIT Press.
Kilborn, Richard and John Izod (1997). *Confronting Reality: An Introduction to Television Documentary*. Manchester: Manchester University Press.
Latour, Bruno (2005a). *Reassembling the Social: An Introduction to Actor Network Theory*. Oxford: Oxford University Press.
Latour, Bruno (2005b). From realpolitik to dingpolitik or how to make things public. In Bruno Latour and Peter Wiebel, eds. *Making Things Public: Atmospheres of Democracy*, 14-41. Cambridge, MA: MIT Press.
Latour, Bruno and Woolgar, Steve (1986). *Laboratory Life: The Construction of Scientific Facts*. New Jersey: Princeton University Press.
Law, John (2004). *After Method: Mess in Social Science Research*. London: Routledge.
Lawrence, Michael and Karen Lury (2016). Introduction: images of exhibition and encounter. In Michael Lawrence and Karen Lury, eds. *The Zoo and Screen Media: Images of Exhibition and Encounter*, v-xiv. New York: Palgrave Macmillan.
Lestel, Dominique, Jeffery Bussolini and Matthew Chrulew (2014). The phenomenology of animal life. *Environmental Humanities* 5: 125-48.
Leung, Chee Chee (2007). Boffins lobby ABC on unit. *The Age*, 15 September. https://tinyurl.com/mrxmyux2.
Lezaun, Javier, Fabian Muniesa and Signe Vikkelsø (2013). Provocative containment and the drift of social-scientific realism. *Journal of Cultural Economy* 6(3) 278-93.
Lippit, Akira Mizuta (2000). *Electric Animal: Toward a Rhetoric of Wildlife*. Minneapolis: University of Minnesota Press.
Look and Listen Magazine (1985). Frogs – a man and his obsession. 7 May. No author.
Lorimer, Jamie (2015). *Wildlife in the Anthropocene: Conservation After Nature*. Minneapolis: Minnesota University Press.
Lorimer, Jamie (2010). Moving image methodologies for more-than-human geographies. *Cultural Geographies* 17(2): 237-58.

References

Lorimer, Jamie (2007). Nonhuman charisma. *Environment and Planning D: Society and Space* 25(5): 911–32.

Louson, Eleanor (2018). Taking spectacle seriously: wildlife film and the legacy of natural history display. *Science in Context* 31(5): 15–38.

Lynch, Michael (2005). The production of scientific images: vision and re-vision in the history, philosophy, and sociology of science. In Luc Pauwels, ed. *Visual Cultures of Science: Rethinking Representational Practices in Knowledge Building and Science Communication*, 26–40. Chicago: University of Chicago Press.

Mangan, Lucy (2019). Our Planet review: Attenborough's first act as an eco-warrior. *Guardian*, 5 April. https://tinyurl.com/y9yk92w9.

Marres, Noortje and Javier Lezaun (2011). Materials and devices of the public: an introduction. *Economy and Society* 40(4): 489–509.

McMahon, Laura and Michael Lawrence (2015). Introduction: animal life and the moving image. In Michael Lawrence and Laura McMahon, eds. *Animal Life and the Moving Image*, 1–18. London: Bloomsbury.

Michael, Mike (2017). *Actor-Network Theory: Trials, Trails, Tribulations*. London: Sage.

Michael, Mike (2009). Publics performing publics: of PiGs, PiPs, and politics. *Public Understanding of Science* 8(5): 617–31.

Mills, Brett (2010). Television wildlife documentaries and animals' right to privacy. *Continuum: Journal of Media and Cultural Studies* 24(2): 193–202.

Mitman, Gregg (2009). *Reel Nature: America's Romance with Wildlife on Film*. Seattle: University of Washington Press.

Mol, Annemarie (1999). *The Body Multiple: Ontology in Medical Practice*. Durham, NC: Duke University Press.

Monbiot, George (2018). David Attenborough has betrayed the living world he loves. *Guardian*, 7 November. https://tinyurl.com/ye2mhdev.

Mulvey, Laura (2006). *Death 24x a Second: Stillness and the Moving Image*. London: Reaktion Books.

Muniesa, Fabian (2014). *The Provoked Economy: Economic Reality and the Performative Turn*. London: Routledge.

Nessel, Sabine (2012). The media animal: On the mise-en-scène of animals in the zoo and cinema. In Sabine Nessel, Winfried Pauleit, Christine Rüffert, Karl-Heinz Schmid and Alfred Tews, eds. *Animals and the Cinema: Classifications, Cinephilias, Philosophies*, 33–48. Berlin: Bertz and Fischer.

Neyland, Daniel and Catelijne Coopmans (2014). Visual accountability. *The Sociological Review* 62(1): 1–23.

Nichols, Bill (1991). *Representing the Reality: Issues and Concepts in Documentary*. Bloomington: Indiana University Press.
Northern Pictures (2021). *Great Barrier Reef*. Press Kit.
Northern Pictures (2020). *After the Fires*. Press Kit.
O'Regan, Tom and Huw Walmsley-Evans (2016). The film reviewing of Kenneth Slessor: a cine-aesthetics of the sound cinema. *Studies in Australasian Cinema* 10(2): 211–22.
Paddle, Robert (2000). *The Last Tasmanian Tiger: The History and Extinction of the Thylacine*. Cambridge: Cambridge University Press.
Paine, Barry (2002). *Dione Gilmour: Oral History Transcript*. University of Bristol, Wild Film Archive, DM2911.
Parer, David (no date). "Post Production Film Script – *Wildlife of Papua New Guinea: The Immigrant Deer*". ABC NHU Archive, Box 11/1427, no page numbers.
Parer, David (no date). "Field Notes". ABC NHU Archive, Box 11/1427, no page numbers.
Pauwels, Luc (2005). A theoretical framework for assessing visual representational practices in knowledge building and science communications. In Luc Pauwels, ed. *Visual Cultures of Science: Rethinking Representational Practices in Knowledge Building and Science Communication*, 1–25. Chicago: University of Chicago Press.
Pick, Anat (2015a). Animal life in the cinematic Umwelt. In Michael Lawrence and Laura McMahon, eds. *Animal Life and the Moving Image*, 221–37. London and New York: Palgrave, on behalf of the British Film Institute.
Pick, Anat (2015b). Why not look at animals? *NECSUS: European Journal of Media Studies* 4(1): 107–25.
Pick, Anat (2007). Ecovisions: seeing animals in recent ethnographic film. *Vertigo Magazine* 3(4). https://tinyurl.com/37dp9sfu.
Pick, Anat and Guinevere Narraway, eds (2013). *Screening Nature: Cinema Beyond the Human*. New York and Oxford: Berghahn.
Pyne, Stephen J. (2021). *The Pyrocene*. Berkeley: University of California Press.
Richards, Morgan (2013). Global nature global brand: BBC Earth and David Attenborough's landmark wildlife series. *Media International Australia* 146: 143–54.
Robin, Libby (1994). *Defending the Little Desert: The Rise of Ecological Consciousness in Australia*. Melbourne: Melbourne University Press.
Robin, Libby (2007). Living with lyrebirds. *Kunapipi* 29(2) 126–34. http://ro.uow.edu.au/kunapipi/vol29/iss2/9.

References

Rowe, David, Graeme Turner and Emma Waterton, eds (2018). *Making Culture: Commercialisation, Transnationalism, and the State of "Nationing" in Contemporary Australia*. London: Routledge.

Simpson, Catherine (2010). Australian eco-horror and Gaia's revenge: animals, eco-nationalism and the "new nature". *Studies in Australasian Cinema* 4(1) 43–54.

Sleightholme, Stephen (2011). Confirmation of the gender of the last captive Thylacine. *Australian Zoologist* 35(4): 953–6.

Sleightholme, Stephen and Cameron Campbell (2015). The earliest motion picture footage of the last captive thylacine? *Australian Zoologist* 37(3): 282–7.

Smaill, Belinda (2014). Documentary film and animal modernity in *Raw Herring* and *Sweetgrass*. *Australian Humanities Review* 57: 61–80.

Smaill, Belinda (2015). Tasmanian tigers and polar bears: the documentary moving image and (species) loss. *NECSUS: European Journal of Media Studies* 4(1): 145–62.

Smaill, Belinda (2020). Historicising David Attenborough's nature: nation, continent, country and environment. *Celebrity Studies* 13(3): 344–65.

Stengers, Isabelle (2008). A constructivist reading of process and reality. *Theory, Culture and Society* 25(4): 91–110.

Sun (1926). On The Trail of the 'Roo. NSW, 9 April, 11.

Sydney Morning Herald (1926). On the Trail of the 'Roo. Sydney, 9 April, 7.

Sydney Morning Herald (1988). 1988: The restless year. 5 December, 69.

Taylor, Ken (1976). Natural History Filming in Australia. Paper presented at the *British Kinematograph, Sound and Television Society's First International Wildlife Film Makers' Symposium*, Slimbridge, Gloucestershire, England, 26–29 February. ABC NHU Archive, Box 10/5418.

Teurlings, Jan (2013). From the society of the spectacle to the society of the machinery: mutations in popular culture 1960s–2000s. *European Journal of Communication* 28(5): 514–26. https://doi.org/10.1177/0267323113494077.

Thrift, Nigel (2007). *Non Representational Thinking: Space, Politics, Affect*. London and New York: Routledge.

Thomas, Laurie (1972). Spotlight on the untouched Australia. *Australian*, 16 May.

Tuan, Yi-Fu (1984). *Dominance and Affection: The Making of Pets*. New Haven, CT: Yale University Press.

Turner, Graeme (1993). *Nation, Culture, Text: Australian Cultural and Media Studies*. London: Routledge.

Van Dooren, Thom and Deborah Bird Rose (2017). Encountering a more-than-human world: ethos and the arts of witness. In Ursula Heise, Jon Christensen and Michelle Neimann, eds. *The Routledge Companion to the Environmental Humanities*, 120–8. Abingdon: Routledge.

Vandenbeld, John (1984). The nature of Australia: aims. ABC NHU Archive, Box 12/4751.
Vandenbeld, John (1988). *Nature of Australia: A Portrait of the Island Continent*. Sydney: Harper Collins/Australian Broadcasting Corporation.
Virilio, Paul (1997). *Open Sky*. Julie Rose, trans. London: Verso.
Warner, Michael (2002). *Publics and Counterpublics*. New York: Zone Books.
Weekly Times (1953). Disney nature film. Melbourne, 14 January, 52. No author.
Wilkie, Alex (2018). Speculating. In Celia Lury, Rachel Fensham, Alexandra Heller-Nicholas, Sybille Lammes, Angela Last, et al., eds. *Routledge Handbook of Interdisciplinary Research Methods*, 347–51. London: Routledge.
Winthrop-Young, Geoffrey (2013). Cultural techniques: preliminary remarks. *Theory, Culture and Society* 30(6): 3–19.
Wolfe, Cary (2017). Ecologizing biopolitics, or, what is the "bio-" of bioart? In Eric Hörl, ed., with James Burton. *General Ecology: The New Ecological Paradigm*, 217–34. London: Bloomsbury Academic.
Wright, Tony (1988). Australia is the star of this show. *Canberra Times*, 28 May.

Index

Aboriginal people 21, 57, 66, 122, 129–131, 136, 141
  agency 126
  dispossession 130, 132
  knowledge 135
  time 135
access 25, 57, 67, 75, 77, 81, 87, 95, 107, 112, 141, 154, 166, 168, 171
accounting for animals 18, 24, 49, 64, 83–87, 91, 163
advocacy 173
aesthetics of natural performances 17, 64
affect
  affective community 111
  affective impacts 146
  affective micropolitics 147
  affective responses 27
Alaimo, Stacy 157
amateur naturalists 49, 52, 74
American Museum of Natural History 30
Anderson, Benedict 128

animal bodies 12, 26, 30, 32, 41, 44, 82, 99, 105, 110, 110, 164
animal disappearance 6, 31, 36, 41, 42, 141, 149
animal performances 4, 7–9, 16, 18, 19, 24, 30, 41, 43, 48, 49, 56, 66, 68, 74, 83, 96, 100, 102, 102, 105, 113, 164, 166, 170, 174
animal studies 6, 9, 14, 167
animality 9, 163
animals
  as authentic 10, 12, 19, 74, 75, 84, 99, 113, 164
  as celebrities 55, 63
  as companion species 15, 146, 166
  as devices of the public 5, 22, 46, 47, 64, 66, 163
  as entertainment 4, 16, 40, 41, 42, 44, 48, 89, 90, 173
  as public things 4, 22
  as subjects 103, 111, 115, 166
  disposable animal body 32
  domesticated 10, 18, 19, 20, 69, 90, 95, 97, 104, 106, 110

electric 6, 13
hunted 16, 30, 38, 42
imprinted 10, 20, 90, 103, 104, 109, 114
informative 49, 87, 92, 165
manipulations of 90, 113
mediated 2, 6, 7, 12, 19, 23, 25, 26, 61, 91, 102, 164, 165, 167
natural history 2–7, 10, 12, 13, 15, 17–24, 25–28, 45–47, 67–70, 71–74, 80–83, 86–88, 90–92, 93, 95, 100, 103, 112, 166, 167, 169, 170
political 1, 24, 163, 165, 166, 167
sonic 49
technical 6
televisual 1–16, 18, 24, 25, 26, 28, 48, 51, 53–55, 62, 66, 67, 68, 69, 77, 78, 81, 83, 84, 90, 96, 97, 101, 102, 106, 110, 113, 116, 124, 163, 164, 165, 167, 174
textual 6
wild 9, 74
working 20, 48, 69, 93, 95, 97, 100, 103, 111–113
Antarctica 76
Anthropocene 135
anthropocentric 72, 84, 91, 146, 157, 158, 159, 171
anthropomorphic 3, 9
archival research 23
Argonauts Club 48
"The Muddle-Headed Wombat" 48
Argus 39
Around the Bush 58
art 83
artists 19
assemblage 19
Atlantic Productions 20, 68

Attenborough, David 6, 17, 47, 101, 144, 145, 149, 161; *see also* Your Planet
David Attenborough's Conquest of the Skies 20, 68
Life on Earth 145
"The Making of David Attenborough's Conquest of the Skies" 20, 68, 69, 94–114
Zoo Quest 47, 52–56
"Zoo Quest For a Dragon" 53
attunement 62, 109, 110, 111
audiences 2–8, 13, 15–17, 20, 22–28, 30, 44, 45–48, 50–53, 56, 57, 59, 60, 63, 67, 69, 70, 74, 80, 85, 87–90, 94, 96, 97, 100, 106, 107, 112, 116, 117, 122, 123, 124, 126, 127, 128, 138, 139, 140, 141, 145, 146, 147, 150–153, 163–166, 168–174
Australia Today 58
Australian Broadcasting Commission (ABC) 2–9, 14–19, 45–52, 56, 71, 74, 85, 87, 91, 119, 124, 125, 137, 137, 138, 139, 164, 165, 166, 168, 169
ABC *Annual Reports* 45
ABC archives 8, 19
ABC Charter 3, 119
Australian Conservation Foundation 137
Australian Heritage Commission 121
Australian nature 4
Australian Reptile Park 49
Australian Screen 124

Bagust, Phil 10, 11
Barthes, Roland 34
Barton, Edmund 129
Bazin, André 34
Beaumaris Zoo 16, 29

Index

Bennett, Tony 27
Berger, John 30–32, 44
Bergson, Henri 154, 158
bicentenary 5, 119
big optics 157
biological 21
Black Summer fires 142
blue chip 68, 124, 132, 136, 145, 169
Blue Planet 145
Bousé, Derek 10, 11
Bowker, Geoffrey 78
Boyde, Melissa 27
British Broadcasting Corporation (BBC) 2, 3, 17, 47, 48, 51, 52, 55, 56, 57, 67, 74, 121–126, 138, 144, 145, 149
Bruun Jensen, Casper 174
Buck, Rose 103
Bush Quest with Robin Hill 64

camera 7, 16, 17, 25, 26, 27, 29, 33, 34, 36, 37, 38, 41, 42, 47, 50, 54, 60, 61, 62, 74, 75, 77, 79, 80, 81, 85, 89, 101, 102, 103–104, 107, 107, 110, 113, 114, 143, 147, 155, 156, 159, 160, 161
captivation 16, 43
capture 5, 8, 14, 16, 17, 22, 25, 26, 37, 43, 47, 64, 73, 78, 99
Channel 10 51
  Animal World 51
Channel 7 50
  Kingdom of the Sea 50
Channel 9 51
  Skippy the Bush Kangaroo 51
  The Shark Hunters 51
  Zoorama 51
charisma 55
Chauvel, Charles and Elsa 56
  Australian Walkabout 56

Chisholm, Alec 49
Chow, Rey 26
cinematic *dispositif* 100
citizen-viewers 23
civic interest and engagement 45
climate change 20, 21, 133, 138, 139, 148, 150, 152, 174
co-fabrication 108
collaboration 108
Collard, Rosemary-Claire 32
collective political engagement 172
colonialism 44, 129, 130, 131
  colonial nature 60, 65
  colonial power 4
  colonial violence 132
Colossus Productions 20, 68
common world 16
companions 166
compositional 109
conservation 5, 19, 44, 57, 58, 64, 83, 87, 132, 140, 149, 151, 172, 173
contact zones 2, 24, 48, 96
containment 8, 16, 17, 18, 29, 35, 110, 111
Coopmans, Catelijne 106
co-present immediacy 152
coral 139
  spawning 139, 153
  bleaching 140
cosmo-ecological alliances 174
Couldry, Nick 12
co-viewing experiences 152
Craig, John D. 50
CSIRO 49, 58
cultural authority 84
cultural codes 72
cultural nationalism 124
cultural techniques 3, 8
curiosity 7, 16, 23, 44, 53, 54, 61, 62, 67, 84, 168, 172, 173

Dalton, Kim 137
Dancing Orpheus 17, 60–64
   Spotty 63
Darwin, Charles 122
Davis, Therese 129, 158
death 149
deep time 127, 157
Despret, Vinciane 7, 110, 111, 165
diminished human agency 148
direct observation 69
direct witnessing 62
Disney 1, 50
   True-Life Adventure 50
documentary realism 62
Dorward, Douglas 65, 82
duration 131, 154, 158, 160, 161

early Australian screen culture 16
earthly multitudes 150
earth-systems processes 116
ecology
   denaturalisation of ecologies 148
   ecological collapse 139
   ecological consciousness 59
   ecological interconnectedness 145
   ecological nationalism 120
   ecological recovery 143
   restoration ecology 149
eco-media 5
editing 10
education 17
elemental forces 143
embodiment 161
emotive witnessing 26
empathy 111, 146
end of nature 174
entangled modes of existence 166
environmental awareness 171
environmental citizens 166, 171
environmental history 83, 143

environmental movements 171
environmental nationalism 47, 56, 58, 60, 66
environmental politics 57, 171, 173
epistemological practices 74
epistemophilia 91
ethical registers 139
ethical witnessing 147
ethology 74
Eurocentricity 131
European invasion 129
evidence of entrapment 25
evidential value 68
exhibitionary afterlife 43, 44
exhibitionary complex 27, 30, 40, 41, 56, 168
exhibitionary practices 1
exploitation 1, 24, 57, 132, 167, 171, 172
Exploration North 168
expository content 141
extinction 16, 29, 34, 43, 134, 139, 140, 143, 147, 174
extreme storms 140

fabrication 9, 10
factitious 7, 98
Fauna Productions 51
field work 75
filmmakers 19
fire 130, 135, 142–150
First Nations 21
Fleay, David 32
fossil fuels 143
Friends of the ABC 137
Frith, Harry 58
Frow, John 71, 79, 169

Gaia 145, 149

Index

genre 9, 18, 19, 24, 30, 51, 52, 62, 68, 70, 71–75, 78–79, 83–88, 90, 91, 93, 102, 102, 106, 108, 111, 121, 140, 144, 146, 157, 161, 168–171
geological history 126
geology 21
Gilmour, Dione 88, 122, 125, 126
global environmental imagination 145
globalisation 133
Gondwana 131
Gouyon, Jean-Baptiste 67, 74, 75, 102
Great Barrier Reef Marine Park Authority 87
greylag geese 109
grief 141

Haraway, Donna 157
Hawkins, Desmond 52
The Naturalist 52
Heise, Ursula 140, 157
Hellmrich Conrad Ltd 39
Hepp, Andreas 12, 13
hide 80
Hill, Robin 64, 123
Hocking, Kevin 122
Holden, Karina 151
Horak, Jan-Christopher 29
human
  affects 16, 109
  as sovereign 27; *see also* sovereign humans
  detachment 80
  human–animal contact zones 48
  human–animal relations 3
  more-than-human publics 24, 109
  more-than-human temporal scale 159
  observation 16
  ontological security 146
  scale 146
hunt films 29

ideological modes of vision 15
immersive spectatorship 145
imprinting 106, 109, 109, 111, 113
indexicality 35, 74, 99
infrastructures of communication 14
inhabitation 16, 20, 22, 115, 116, 125, 127, 130, 132, 134, 135, 136, 157
inscription devices 11, 12, 73, 104
institutional practices 23
insurance populations 149
interspecies intimacy 52
intra-action 79
Izod, John 94

Jue, Melody 175

Kangaroo Island 143
kangaroos 16, 29, 32, 39, 40, 59, 143, 172, 173
Kember, Sarah 151, 154, 158, 160
Kilborn, Richard 94
"Kinchega: Under New Management" 172

laboratory 81, 89, 90, 135
land clearing 143
Lassie 51
Latour, Bruno 10, 12, 104
Law, John 11, 12
learning to be affected 28
Lestel, Dominique 163
Lezaun, Javier 5, 17, 46, 98, 112, 167
Lippit, Akira Mizuka 6, 13, 31, 32, 34
live/life tension 154
living earth 145
Logies 123
logoization of space 128
Look 3, 52
Lorenz, Konrad 109
The Ethology of the Greylag Goose 109

Lorimer, Jamie 26, 55
Louson, Eleanor 91
Lumière brothers 30
Lynch, Michael 19

Macdonald, Hamish 153, 156
making-of documentaries (MODs) 68, 93–114
　dynamics of staging 95
Marres, Noortje 5, 46
mass animal death 146
matters of concern 23, 24, 172
McDonagh sisters 32
McGown, Edward 101
meaning-making 11
media studies 5, 9, 10, 13, 77, 96, 113, 154
mediation 1, 8–15, 74–83, 160
　mediated vitality 6
　mediatisation 8, 13, 14
megafires 142–150
　Black Summer fires 142, 143
Melbourne Symphony Orchestra 122
Melbourne Zoo 123
modernity 129, 133
Monbiot, George 6
moral capacities 46
multiplying worlds 165
multispecies encounter 166, 167, 169, 173
multispecies plurality 7
Mulvey, Laura 34
Muniesa, Fabian 98, 99, 100, 112
museums 1, 14, 168

narration of nation 129
narrative framings 81
Narraway, Guinevere 101
nation 5, 20, 21, 50, 125, 128
national animals 59, 65

national broadcaster *see* Australian Broadcasting Commission (ABC)
national culture 2, 4
national identity 4, 23, 24
national imaginary 125, 126
national interest 46
national patrimony 115, 133
national progress 44
national time 21, 126, 127, 129, 131, 132, 134
national value 46
nationalism 47, 56, 58, 60, 124, 131
nationalist politics 57
nationing 21, 116, 124
nationing natural history 116, 119, 125–136
Natural History Unit (NHU) 4, 18, 65, 67, 88, 90, 119, 168, 169, 170
　BBC's NHU 67, 124
　closure 137
natural purity 64
natural resilience 143, 161
natural sciences 27
naturalists 3
nature as purified 5, 166
nature 6, 20, 21, 58, 61, 67, 69, 75, 79, 83, 85, 93, 101, 102, 124, 126, 130, 133, 138, 141, 142, 150, 151, 152, 153, 159, 160, 163, 166, 168, 169, 170, 171, 174
nature films or shows 3, 17
Nature of Australia 5, 20, 119
　"A Separate Creation" 122
　"End of Isolation" 133
nature/culture distinction 150
News from Nature 48
newspapers 14
newsreel 3
Neyland, Daniel 106
Nguyen, Jordan 153

Index

nonhuman animals 7, 97
noninterference 75
Northern Pictures 21, 138, 151

objectivity 69
observational realism 74
ocular inflation 101
Olsen, John 65, 66, 85
ontological orientation 8, 9, 12, 24, 27, 35, 36, 62, 74, 75, 78, 79, 91, 97, 100, 146
outback, the 20, 56, 58, 60

Paine, Barry 125
Panda Awards 123
Papua New Guinea 76
Parer, David 19, 68, 75–83, 122
 Wildlife of Papua New Guinea 19, 68, 76
 "The Immigrant Deer" 76
pastoral capitalism 32
Pauwels, Luc 73
pedagogic purposes 24, 83
performativity 8, 11, 12, 15, 17, 22, 96, 108, 158, 159, 164, 166
Phillip, Arthur 129
Pick, Anat 62, 72, 95, 100, 101
Pizzey, Graham 58
Planet Earth 145
planet 20, 21
 planetarity 148
 planetary agency 150
 planetary cultural imaginary 158
 planetary event 150
 planetary interconnectedness 115
 planetary limit 149
 sense of planet 21, 115, 140, 141, 142, 145, 147, 148, 150, 153, 157, 161
PNG Wildlife Division 87
 The Bird of the Thunderwoman 87

popularising science 86
post natural history 139
post-colonial 125, 132, 135
post-representational 97
presentism 155
pre-televisual 16, 26
processes of modernisation 57
provocative containment 35, 98, 99
provoking 15, 18, 19, 23, 42, 43, 46, 47, 55, 67, 69, 70, 74, 79, 81, 84, 88–92, 95, 97, 103, 107, 109, 110, 112, 113, 165, 166, 167
public broadcasting 3, 8, 13, 17, 26, 45, 48, 50, 74, 163, 168
public circulation 15, 16
public concerns 2, 3, 9, 20, 46, 60, 66, 166, 167
public interest 4, 16, 22, 23
public value 4, 22, 23
publics 2, 8, 9, 15, 16, 22, 23, 24, 166
 modes of publicness 16, 23, 24, 165
purified natures 5, 166
Pyrocene 144

radio 2, 3, 14, 47–52, 58, 122
realism 11, 61, 62, 74, 95, 99, 100, 112, 164
reality effects 12, 15, 67, 69, 71, 79, 99
reconstruction 10
Reef Live 21, 138, 139, 141, 150–162
referent 19, 32, 35, 139, 150, 174
reflexivity 95, 97
 reflexive mode 94
regimes of value 43, 83
Reid, Arthur 36
remediation 47, 50
renewal of life 152, 153
representational burden 7
responsibility to care 64, 115, 147, 173
Rettig, Neil 122

Richards, Morgan 144
Robin, Libby 59
Ron Taylor Productions 51
Roosevelt, Theodore 30
   Roosevelt in Africa 30
Rose, Deborah Bird 146, 147
rusa deer 76

sacrificing 173
safari format 56
Satchwell, Brooke 153, 156
science 5, 27, 39, 55, 58, 64, 82, 83, 85, 86, 87, 88, 90, 91, 102, 111, 113, 135, 141, 145, 152, 161, 162, 173
science and technology studies (STS) 9, 11, 12, 13, 14, 46, 73, 81, 96, 99, 108, 112, 113
Science Commentary 49
scientific facts 4, 7, 20, 69, 82, 86, 89, 90, 91, 95, 97, 102–105, 106, 109, 111, 141, 144, 146, 152, 156, 169
scientific objectivity 36
scientific positivism 64
scientists 19, 65, 68, 87, 88, 89, 90, 91, 135, 137, 141, 146, 165, 172, 174
scopophilia 91
screen studies 9, 14, 96, 112, 113
Scully, William 132
sense of dwelling 115
Serventy, Vincent 58
settler programs of extermination 32
settler-national 4
settler-state 125
shared vulnerability 147
show and tell 56, 91, 126, 168
signification 11
Simpson, Catherine 36
Sky TV 20, 68
Slessor, Kenneth 38
Smaill, Belinda 35, 129, 145, 158, 159

social figurations 14
society of the machinery 93
sociobiological containment 110
sociotechnical practices 25, 46, 74, 79, 80, 83, 99, 101, 107, 109, 111, 163, 175
sovereign humans 15, 27, 47, 48, 56, 165, 166, 168, 169, 175
spatial scale 159–161
species decline 6
spectacle 30, 41–43, 45, 53, 91, 112, 153, 155, 159, 173
spectral beasts 31, 33–43
spontaneous self-betrayal 47
spoonbills 77
stranger sociability 111

Taylor, Ken 59, 65, 86, 87, 125
technical practices and vision 6, 8, 9, 12, 15, 47, 50, 54, 62, 65, 69, 70, 73, 77, 93, 94, 95, 101, 102, 106, 107, 110, 113, 114, 126, 153, 157, 159
   3D 101, 103, 104, 107, 114
   computer-generated imagery (CGI) 141, 153
   God trick 157
   hidden camera 62
   simulation 5, 11, 153
   soundtracks 10
   special effects 5, 10
   stock footage 10, 153
technogenesis 93
telephoto lens 29
television 14, 93
   blockbuster 145
temporal colonisation 132
Teurlings, Jan 69, 93
textual effects 72
The Man Who Loves Frogs 88–90
The Trail of the 'Roo 16, 29

Index

The World We Share 168
thylacine 16
"the last Tasmanian tiger" 37
traditional knowledge 135
trans-corporeal merging 161
Troughten, Ellis 49
Tyler, Michael 88; *see also The Man Who Loves Frogs*

umwelt 41, 100
uncanny, the 34
underwater immersive experience 160
Untamed World 50
urbanisation 143

Van Dooren, Thom 146, 147
Vandenbeld, John 119, 120, 121–123, 126, 169, 170
Victorian Forestry Commission 87
Wildfire 87
Vikkelsø, Signe 98
virtual witnessing 69
visual conquest of nature 157
visual languages 81
visual mastery 62
vitality of media 151

Wake in Fright 82
Weaving, Hugo 143
Where Angels Swim 87

white settlement 21
whooper swans 69, 97, 98, 101–114
Wild Australia 65, 76
Wild Australia: After the Fires 21, 138
Wild Australia: Beyond the Dunes 85
Wild Australia: The Southern Edge 168
Wild Life Paradise: Australian Fauna 58
Wilderness Society 137
Wild-life and the Countryman 49
Wildlife Australia 58
Wilkie, Alex 107
Williams, Robyn 122
Wolfe, Cary 148
Woolgar, Steve 104
Worrell, Eric 49
Wright, Judith 66

Your Planet 21, 138
Big Weather: And How to Survive It 21, 138
David Attenborough: Extinction 138

zoo films 29
zookeepers 29
zoological specimen 41
zoologists 29
zoomorphic realism 100
zoos 1
Zylinska, Joanna 151, 154

www.ingramcontent.com/pod-product-compliance
Lightning Source LLC
Chambersburg PA
CBHW042137160426
43200CB00020B/2968